The Ultimate Dachshund Hound Book

Guide to Caring, Raising, Training, Breeding,
Whelping, Feeding, and Loving a Doxie

Patricia O'Grady

authorHOUSE®

AuthorHouse™
1663 Liberty Drive
Bloomington, IN 47403
www.authorhouse.com
Phone: 1-800-839-8640

First published by AuthorHouse 6/14/2010

ISBN: 978-1-4520-3254-2 (e)
ISBN: 978-1-4520-3252-8 (sc)
ISBN: 978-1-4520-3253-5 (hc)

Library of Congress Control Number: 2010908245

Printed in the United States of America
Bloomington, Indiana

This book is printed on acid-free paper.

"To those who claim that money can't buy love or happiness, I say they forgot about Doxie puppies"

This book is dedicated to Heidi and Bingo.

Table of Contents

The Delightful Dachshund

The Dachshund is a delightful, intelligent, lovable, active, and loyal breed of dog which has no problem fitting into just about any type of household. They only require moderate exercise, and can adapt easily to small apartment living. They are strictly an inside pet, and should never be left to live outdoors. They can be an ideal family pet for families with children as long as the children understand how to treat the dog. They make a perfect companion, warm and affectionate, yet will serve as a wonderful watchdog, never failing to let you know that someone has invaded their property with a loud bark.

When someone new comes to visit your home, a Dachshund will usually stand back from them, observing the new arrival from a safe distance, until their affections have finally been won over. Once you have made a friend of them, they will be a friend for life and will remember that person the next time they come to visit.

You can't help but love this friendly, playful little dog with how they manage to use their darling facial expressions and how they just seem to have a way of speaking to you with their expressive eyes. They enjoy interaction with their owners, and love attention showered on them by people. You can expect them to roll on their backs for a tummy rub when guests arrive, and wag their tail with excitement, as they have a way of demanding attention when they feel they aren't getting enough of it.

These adorable dogs have been given several different nicknames, the most common ones being, doxies, dashies, teckel, wiener dogs, sausage dogs, and hot dogs, due to the obvious shape of their long body.

This breed was made for hunting therefore you'll find it has a keen sense of smell, and the AKC lists them in the hound group. They are widely known for their long and low bodies, and are easily recognized. They are eager to hunt and will excel in above and below ground searches.

This was a very popular breed in the early 1900's but sadly due to the First World War, and negativity with anything associated with being of German origin, these dogs lost much of their popularity, but they have made a strong comeback due to the efforts of dedicated breeders in the past decade. The Dachshund are now one of the most popular breeds owned in the United States according to the AKC Registration Statistics, being listed somewhere in the top 7 breeds for the last few years.

Many Doxie owners will have more than one, because caring for two isn't much more work, and they delight in the company of each other.

Doxie's come in three different coat varieties, Smooth, Wirehaired or Longhaired, although the smooth haired coat seems to be the most popular. The smooth coat requires no grooming, while the other two coats will need regular grooming sessions.

This breed comes in two different sizes, the Miniature size weighs 11 pounds or less, and the standard size can be up to 32 pounds full grown.

Dachshunds sport a charming personality and you can expect them to use their strong head to nudge your hand when wanting to be acknowledged and petted. They are extremely intelligent, and you must establish that you are their boss, not the other way around, but once the roles are set, you will have a courageous, clever and loving pet.

This breed can suffer from separation anxiety more than some of the other breeds, and requires a great deal of human companionship. They dislike being left alone for more than a few hours, so if you work all day, this is probably not the best breed for you, unless you are able to stop home during your lunch hour to reassure your dog. You can always expect your Doxie to greet you at the door, welcoming your arrival back home.

The Origin of the Dachshund

The Dachshund is a very old breed and drawings of it have been traced in history all the way back to the 15th century. The breed clearly originated in Germany. The name Dachshund comes from two German words, "Dachs" which means badger and "Hund" which has the meaning of hound. Illustrations have been discovered showing badgers being hunted with dogs that had elongated bodies, short little legs, and hound type long ears. These dogs from medieval Europe had the tracking ability of larger hounds yet the proportions and fearless temperament of a terrier, which was much needed in order to pursue their quarry of badgers. German foresters needed to develop a small sturdy hunting dog breed that was capable of tracking thru thick undergrowth and even underground, and was built for fitting into narrow burrows to capture badgers, which was considered to be a major pest at the time. Anyone that owns a Dachshund can tell you that although they have short legs, this breed is certainly able to cover land at great speed, and also has a loud bark to let the hunters stay on their trail.

Sometime in the 17th century, the breed had the smooth short coat, and the longhaired coat varieties, with the wirehair being added later in 1890. The original German breeders learned that crossing longhairs, with smoothes or wirehairs harmed the breed, and barred any such crossed breeding from registration.

It is thought that the French Braque (a small pointer type) and the Pinscher were used to develop the smooth-haired Dachshund. We also know thru history that the German's bred the original Dachshund to French Bassets, and those puppies would have resulted into Dachsbracke, if they possessed long legs, and Dachshunds if they had shorter legs, short ears and pointed muzzles. Although the breed of Dachshund has two different size classes, if should be noted that in Germany there is a third larger size, which they call Kaninchenteckel.

During the course of time in the development of this breed, two different sizes were created based on the type of game being hunted. The dogs that weighed between 30 and 35 pounds were mainly being used to hunt badgers, deer and wild boar, and those that weighed in between 16 – 22 pounds were used to hunt badgers, fox, rabbits and hares.

The Dachshund appeared in the UK around 1840 when Prince Consort received a gift of several smooth haired Dachshunds from Prince Edward of Saxe-Weimar, and the dogs were kept at Windsor and used during pheasant shootings.

The first recorded Dachshund dog show in England was in 1859. The AKC records show that importations into the US happened in 1885. The Dachshund Club of America was finally established in 1895. In 1935 the Dachshund Breed was also added to the AKC field trials in order to encourage hunting capacity and exemplary conformation, along with their wonderful temperament.

Breed Standard

The following is the listing for the AKC breed standard. Please understand that this is very important information if you are planning on placing your dog in the show ring. If you are purchasing a Dachshund for a pet, the following may not be quite as important to you. If a Doxie doesn't completely conform to perfect breed standards in appearance, making it less than show quality, it is called pet quality. When purchased from a good breeder, there can be very little difference between a pet quality and a show quality Doxie. A breeder is looking for puppies that match the exact AKC standards, so that they can categorize their puppy as show or pet quality. All litters, even those puppies that come from champion parents cannot always be all perfect dogs. In many cases, a pet quality puppy has a very small flaw, such as a color mark, or even something slight to the shape of it's ears, or perhaps the dog is a little too small, or too large. If you are looking strictly for just a pet, and have no plans of ever showing your Dachshund, you should consider pet quality, instead of spending the extra money for a show dog. A pet quality Doxie will still be a wonderful companion pet, and you will not love it any less. I would however, always insist on having the AKC registration papers regardless of your pet's quality, even if the papers are limited registration (which means you cannot breed the animal), because this is your only proof that you have purchased a purebred puppy. It's also nice to have the ability to trace your pet's lineage thru the AKC, their documentation of records are flawless.

General Appearance

The Dachshund is part of the hound group. This breed is low to the ground, long in body and should have short legs with strong muscular development. Their skin is expected to be elastic and pliable, but should never have excessive wrinkling. The breed should never appear to be awkward, cramped in capacity for its movement or crippled in anyway. The Doxie is well-balanced, and should have a bold and confident head carriage, good intelligence, and expressive facial features.

Known for its hunting spirit, good nose which has an advantage over most breeds for trailing, making it well suited for below ground hunting work, and running thru the bush. It should be noted that since this breed it considered a hunting breed, wounds and scars are not considered a fault for showing.

Size, Proportion and Substance

This breed is bred and shown in two different sizes. The standard and the miniature, which are not separate classifications, however they do complete in a class division which is 11 pounds and under at 12 months of age and older. The weight of the standard size should be between 16 and 32 pounds.

Head & Eyes

When viewed from above or side, the head should taper uniformly to the tip of the nose. The eyes should be medium in size, almond shaped, with dark rims. This breed is expected to have an energetic pleasant expression, and not be piercing or too dark in color. The bridge bones over the eyes are very prominent. A dog with wall eyes, except in the colorings of dappled dogs is considered a serious fault.

The skull is slightly arched, and should not be too broad or too narrow. The skull should slope gradually with a little stop into the finely formed, slightly arched muzzle. The lips are tightly stretched, covering most of the lower jaw area. The nostrils are well open. The jaws opening wide and hinged back to the eyes, with strong developed bones and teeth. The teeth should fit closely together in a scissor bite. An even bite is a minor fault, and any other deviation from the scissor bite considered a serious fault.

Ears

The ears sit near the top of the head, and should not come too far forward. They must be of moderate length, rounded, but not narrow, pointed or folded. When the dog is moving, the forward edge of the ears should just touch the cheek so that they frame the face.

Neck

The Dachshund has a long, muscular, clean cut neck, without dewlap, which is slightly arched in the nape area, flowing gracefully into the shoulder, but should not create the impression of a right angle appearance.

Body

The trunk of the body is long and muscled. When the body is seen in profile, the back lies in a straight line between the withers and the short, very slightly arched loin. A body that hangs loosely between the shoulders is considered a very serious fault. The abdomen should be slightly drawn up.

Forequarters

The front has to be strong, deep, long with clean muscle for effective underground work. The chest breast bone is prominent in front, and a depression or dimple appears on either side. The thorax appears oval and extends downwards to the mid-point of the forearm when the dog is viewed from the front. The ribs appear full and oval. The keel will merge gradually into the line of the abdomen, and should extend well beyond the front legs. The lowest point of the breast line is covered by the front leg when the dog is viewed in a profile position. The shoulder blades are long and broad, well laid back, and placed upon the developed thorax, closely fitted at the withers, with firm muscle. The upper arm is ideally the same length as the shoulder blade, and will right angle to the latter, lying close to the rib area, with elbows close to the body, but very capable of good movement. The forearm is short, and supplied with good muscle on the front and outside, has tightly stretched tendons not only the inside, but also at the back, and slightly curved inwards. The joints between the forearms and the feet are closer together than the shoulder joints. The front does not appear absolutely straight. The inclined shoulder blades, upper arms, and curved forearms should form parentheses that enclose the ribcage, which creates a wraparound front. Make a note that knuckling over is a disqualifying fault in showing. The front paws are tight, compact, with well arched toes, short nails and thick pads. It is considered ok if they are equally inclined in a trifle outward. The front dewclaws may be removed, and I recommend it.

Hindquarters

The hindquarters are strong and muscled. The pelvis, thigh, second thigh and rear pastern are ideally the same length, and should give the appearance of a series of right angles. When viewing from the rear, the thighs are strong and powerful. The legs should not turn in or out. The rear pastern is short yet strong, and perpendicular to the second thigh bone. From the rear view they are upright and parallel. The hind feet paws should be smaller than the front paws, again with short nails, and thick pads. The foot points straight and the dog should stand on the equally balanced on the ball and toe area. The rear dewclaws should always be removed. The tail extends without twists, pronounced curve, or kinks, and should not be too gaily.

Gait

The Doxie Gait is fluid and smooth. The forelegs reach forward, without much life, in unison with the driving action of hind legs. The correct shoulder assembly along with the well-fitted elbows should allow the long, free stride in front. The Doxie viewed from the front, shows that the legs do not move in exact parallel planes, but instead include slightly inward. The hind legs drive on the line with the forelegs, with hock joints and rear pasterns, again with the metatarsus turning neither in nor out. The propulsion of the hind leg depends on the dog's ability to carry the hind leg to complete extension. When viewed in profile, the forward reach of the hind leg equals the rear extension. The thrust of correct movement is seen when the rear pads are clearly exposed during rear extension. Rear feet do not reach upward toward the abdomen and there is no appearance of walking on the rear pasterns. The feet must travel parallel to the line of motion with no tendency to swing out, cross over, or interfere with each other. Short, choppy movement, rolling or high-stepping gait, close or overly wide coming or going are incorrect. The Dachshund must show that it has agility, freedom of movement, and endurance to do the work for which he was developed.

Temperament

The Dachshund is clever, lively and courageous to the point of rashness, persevering in above- and below-ground work, with all the senses well-developed. Any display of shyness is a serious fault.

Coat Varieties and Special Characteristics

Dachshunds are bred in three different varieties of coats, Smooth, Wirehaired and Long haired, and also as stated above, show in two different sizes, standard and miniature. All three of the varieties and both of the sizes must conform to the characteristics specified below.

Smooth Dachshund

The Short coat is smooth and shining, and should not be too long or too thick. Long sleek bristles on the underside are considered a patch of strong-growing hair, not a fault. A brush tail is a fault, as is also a partly or wholly hairless tail. Certain patterns and basic colors are predominating.

Solid one colored Dachshunds include red and cream, with or without a shading of interspersed dark hairs. A small amount of white on the chest is acceptable, but not desirable. The nose and nails should always be black in color.

The two colored Dachshunds include black, chocolate, wild boar, grey (blue) and fawn (Isabella), each with deep, rich tan or cream markings, over the eyes, on the sides of the jaw, and under the lip, on the inner edge of the ear, front, breast, and sometimes on the throat, inside and behind the front legs, on the paws and around the anus, and from there to about one-third of one-half of the length of the tail on the underside. Undue prominence of the tan or cream markings is considered undesirable. A small amount of white on the chest is acceptable but not really desirable. The nose and nails in the case of black dogs, should be black; for chocolate and all other colors, dark brown, but self colored is also acceptable.

Dappled Dachshunds (the merle pattern) is expressed as lighter colored areas with contrasting darker base color, which can be any acceptable color. As far as the color, neither the light nor the dark color should be predominating. Partial or wholly blue (wall) eyes are as acceptable as dark eyes. A large area of white on the chest of a dapple is permissible.

The brindle pattern in which black or dark stripes of color occur over the entire body is some specimens that pattern may be visible only in the tan points.

The sable pattern consists of a uniform dark overlay on the red color dogs. The overlay hairs are double pigments, with the tip of each hair much darker than the base color. The pattern usually displays a widow's peak on the head. The nose, nails and eye rims are black, and the darker the eyes color the better.

Wirehaired Dachshunds

The wirehaired Dachshunds coat is cover with a uniform tight, shore, thick, rough, hard, outer coat with finer, somewhat softer shorter hairs (also know as the undercoat), with the exception of the jaw, eyebrows, and ears. The absence of an undercoat is a fault. The distinctive facial furnishings include a beard and eyebrows. On the ears the hair is shorter than on the body, and almost smooth. The general arrangement of the hair is such that the wirehaired Dachshund, when viewed from a distance, resembles the smooth Dachshund. Any sort of soft hair in the outer coat, found on the body or especially on the top of the head is a fault. The same is true of long, curly, or wavy hair, or hair that sticks out irregularly in all directions. The tail is robust, thick haired, gradually tapering to a point. A flag tail is a fault.

The most common colors are wild boar, black and tan, and various shades of red, all colors and patterns listed below are admissible.

The wild boar appears as banding of the individual hairs and imparts an overall grizzled effect. The tan points may or may not be evident. Variations include red boar, and chocolate and tan boar. The nose, and nails and eye rims should be black on the wild boar, and red boar. On the chocolate/tan boar dachshunds, the nose nails and eye rims are self colored, but the darker the better. A small amount of white on the chest is acceptable but not found to be desirable.

Longhaired Dachshund

The longhaired Dachshund has a sleek, glistening, and often slightly wavy hair which is longer under the neck and on the fore chest, the underside of the body, the ears and behind the legs. The coat gives the dog an elegant appearance. Note that short hair on the ears is not desirable. Too profuse a coat which masks type, equally long hair over the whole body, a curly coat or a pronounced parting on the back are also considered faults. The tail is carried gracefully in a prolongation of the spine, the hair attains it greatest length here and form a veritable flag. Acceptable colors and markings are listed below.

Acceptable Colors for all three coats

The following are the acceptable colors for this breed: Black and Cream, Black and Tan, Blue and Cream, Blue and Tan, Chocolate and Cream, Chocolate and Tan, Cream, Fawn & Cream, Fawn & Tan, Red, Wheaten, Wild Boar, Black, Chocolate, Fawn

Acceptable Markings for all three coats

The acceptable markings for this breed is, Brindle, Dapple, Sable, Brindle Piebald, Double Dapple, Piebald.

Where to Purchase a Dachshund Puppy

I always recommend that you purchase your puppy from a private breeder and not a pet store. Pet stores purchase their puppies from puppy mills, and usually have little or no background history of the dogs. It is very unlikely that the puppy's parents were screened for genetic problems that are passed from generation to generation. Most pet shops would like you to believe that since their puppy is registered by the AKC this guarantees the puppy will be healthy. This is not so, the only thing that AKC papers certify is that the puppy is a purebred. Even this can be falsified, as some puppy mills register more puppies than are actually born in each litter to receive extra registration slips to pass out with puppies that came from parents without papers. These puppy mills are in the business to make money; they care little about the breed. The parents of your puppy may be unhealthy or carriers of crippling or deadly health defects which may have been passed to their babies.

You have seen specimens of Doxies in pictures, but this does not guarantee that your puppy will fit the breed standard just because it has papers. You do not know if the parents fit the standard either, and cannot see the faults that each parent has when purchasing from a pet store. A good home breeder will gladly show you the mother and the father (if she owns the stud) and will be willing to discuss the faults and strengths of each of her dogs. Make sure that the mother appears healthy, and hasn't had any post delivery complications, which would mean she didn't care for her puppies and feed them with the proper nutrition. Ask for the medical history of the sires (puppy's father) and dams (puppy's mother).

The puppy that you are buying from a pet store has most likely spent most of its life in a cage. Many pet store puppies have never seen carpet, grass or dirt. Due to the conditions that these puppies are kept in the stores, they have been forced to eliminate in the same area that they sleep and eat. This goes against the dog's natural instinct, but your puppy has had no choice. This habit may make housebreaking your Dachshund much more difficult. A good breeder keeps the puppy area very clean and makes sure the puppy has a separate elimination area. By the time your puppy is ready to go to their new home, it should be on its way to being house trained.

Pups from stores have not been socialized in the same way either, and you will find many of them pull away or simply ignore the hands poking thru the cage that are attempting to pet them. They do not have the same desire or need for human contact, because it is something new or unknown to them. Home breeders handle their puppies more; often giving these puppies' tender loving care, and affection everyday. Since their puppies have been handled lovingly, they are used to the touch, and scent of humans, and understand that it is good. A pet store puppy may have not been in a house before, and everything will be new and scary for them. The sounds of the vacuum cleaner, children playing, the telephone ringing, television, and video games, can all be terrifying to these puppies. Good breeders have their puppies living in their homes with them, not in outside kennels.

Most responsible breeders have also evaluated the temperament of each puppy, and they know which puppies are dominant and which are shy, which is the most energetic, and which is the most passive. Then the breeder can match the puppy to the new owner, making sure that energetic pups go to active families, and the shy ones go to a home that is quieter.

Not all home breeders are good ones either. A good ethical breeder will not cut corners to save a few dollars, their dogs and puppies all see the veterinarian on a regular basis. They know nutrition and make sure that the moms and puppies get the best quality foods and supplements available.

A good breeder will provide you with the name and phone number of their own Veterinarian, because they have nothing to hide. If you are having trouble finding a good Doxie breeder, call around to the local vet's offices because a good breeder is often recommended to future puppy owners by a vet. You can find a breeder at AKC dog shows, usually showing their own Dachshund Hounds. I don't have any problems with calling ads in local newspapers for a puppy, as most of them usually come from wonderful homes, but you must do your homework. Do not be afraid to ask the breeder questions, they should welcome them and be willing to answer them without annoyance. Remember there is no such thing as a stupid question, if you don't know the answer, then you need to ask it.

All Doxie puppies should have had their dewclaws removed by three days old. If this hasn't been done than the breeder is just looking to cut corners and costs, and I would strongly suggest you keep looking elsewhere. You want to purchase a puppy that has been examined by a veterinarian, has had its shots, and been de-wormed, make sure you ask for proof of these things. Each state has different laws and requirements; you should inquire about the laws in your area, and know exactly what the breeder must provide to you. As an example of that, I live in Florida, a state that requires from the breeder to the new owner, a veterinarian signed health certificate, at the time of the puppy sale.

Ask the breeder if they ship their puppies. If the breeder says, yes, run away from them. A breeder, who would ship a puppy alone, is in this for the money and doesn't care about the puppy. Puppies in the cargo department are scared and alone, some have been known to go into shock and die. Still others have gotten lost and stolen, even shipped to the wrong airport, without food or water in their cage for hours. I have heard nightmare stories of puppies freezing on a tarmac treated like a simple piece of luggage, or others that have succumbed from heat exposure. If you have a dog shipped to you, and your dog dies or becomes sick in transport, you cannot request your money back from the breeder because their obligation to you and the puppy ended when the puppy was paid for and dropped off at the airport. If you are unable to locate a local breeder, and must go out of state for your puppy, get in the car, drive and pickup your puppy in person, or get on a plane, and fly back with the puppy on your lap.

There are breeders that will sell Dachshund puppies as young as 8 weeks old, but I don't feel they are ready to be separated from their mother and siblings, and I personally never sent them home to their new families until the pups were 10 weeks old. Separation from their mother at too young an age makes for an insecure puppy.

Another sign of a good breeder is, while you are interviewing them, they should be interviewing you. A good breeder wants to know what kind of home her puppy is going to live in, and how it will be cared for. I didn't breed for the money, and I have turned down people when I didn't want my puppies living in their homes. One story that comes to mind is a man probably in his late 50's. He told me on the phone that he had purchased a puppy but it passed away after one month's time, but he had no idea why the puppy died, and he wanted to replace it. He cursed the store he had purchased it from because they would not give him a refund. After he came to my house, and picked out a puppy, we naturally started to ask each other a few questions. He told me that the puppy he "lost" had been living in his garage, as he didn't believe dogs had a place inside the home. Since we live in Florida, I asked if his garage was air-conditioned and he replied no. I explained to him that in my opinion the reason his puppy most likely died was from heat stroke, because a Florida garage gets very hot during the summer months. I told the stubborn man that he could not allow a dog to live in those terrible conditions. He argued with me that I was wrong, and stated he would be putting the new puppy into the same environment where the other puppy had recently died, which was his business, and not mine. Needless to say, he left my home without a puppy, as I refused to sell him one, and we had an exchange of some heated words. I did go one step further, and called another local breeder in the area, one that I had become friends with, to warn her about this man, so she would refuse to sell him a puppy also. I hope that he wasn't able to purchase another puppy; heat stroke is a terrible death for one to suffer.

Buying a purebred Dachshund is not just about your hard earned money, also your love and emotions are at stake, so please make sure you are buying from a breeder that truly cares about the dogs and isn't in it for just the love of money.

Before you bring your Puppy Home

Y ou have found your Dachshund Hound puppy, and placed a deposit on it. Now is the time to ready the house so you can bring him/her home. All the fun and excitement begins but there are a few things you need to know. You must remember that puppies are just like little children, they are curious and love to snoop around, often getting into everything just to discover what it is, they are learning as they grow. You want your puppy's environment to be safe and secure, and if you do it correctly, your puppy will adjust quicker, learn faster, and in turn you will have less stress, so you'll be able to enjoy your new bundle of joy.

You will first need to purchase the exact same puppy food that the breeder was feeding, please resist from making any changes to your puppies diet for at least one month. Your puppy will also require, two dishes, one for food, one for water, a harness and a leash. I don't recommend that you use a collar on a young Doxie; they can get it lodged on something and easily hang themselves. I recommend that you purchase a dog harness to use and put it on only when they are going outside on the leash; otherwise they don't have it on in the house at all. A harness fits a Doxie's long body perfectly. The harness should also have identification tags. Since Doxie's have a natural tendency to track and chase, you will always want to keep them on a leash for their own safety, this is not a breed that you will train to walk beside you unleashed, without risking it taking off, and those little legs can run faster than you might think.

Other items you are going to need are, a good quality brush, metal comb, (depending on whether you have a long haired or wire haired Doxie) puppy shampoo and conditioner, a soft small blanket, kennel or a cage, a doggie bed, and a few puppy toys. I highly recommend that you invest is a good doggie gate, you don't want to ever give a brand new puppy full run of the house, it's too overwhelming especially for the little ones. Care needs to be given around stairs, a young Doxie puppy, cannot go up and down stairs by itself, this will be something you must teach it, while supervising, so place a doggie gate in front of staircases. Another safe place to put a new puppy is in an old child's playpen, if you have one sitting around or can pick one up at a garage sale, they make the perfect safe environment for your new puppy when you aren't able to keep an eye on them. Things in your home that you would never think about can be a danger to a tiny Dachshund, such as a door closed too quickly, and recliner chairs, so before you do anything, you must always check to see where your puppy is located.

Please walk thru your house before bringing your puppy home to check for the following things listed here. Chances are that your puppy will be a little mischievous and manage to find something to get into eventually, but the things listed here can make your puppy sick or could even be fatal. Make sure that all chemicals are stored away where your Doxie is unable to get to them; this includes household cleaners, bleach, insecticide, pesticide, herbicide, and antifreeze.

All inside houseplants should be removed from the floor. Most people don't realize that puppies will eat the leaves and become ill. Some plants including a Christmas favorite Poinsettia's are toxic to dogs.

Puppies love to chew on dangling electrical cords. Try to rearrange all cords the best that you can, placing them out of your puppies reach. It is important that you keep a close eye on your little curious Dachshund and discipline verbally if you see it is attempting to bite on electrical cords.

Check, and then double check all areas for anything that could fit into your inquisitive puppy's mouth, such as pins, pens, pencils, loose change, medication bottles, or any other possible objects of interest. A new puppy is a like a baby, they want to put everything into their mouths, especially when teething.

Children and Doxie's

Dachshund Hounds make wonderful pets for many homes, however extra care should be given with small children. I don't recommend the smaller breeds to families that have children under the age of 8. Children need to understand that while these breeds seem like toys, they aren't actual toys and rough handling can injure them. Only you know if your child is ready to handle the responsibility that comes with owning a pet, but extra thought must be given when choosing a smaller breed. It is heartbreaking to see one injured because it was mishandled or abused.

Doxies adore children, and will delight in running and playing with them and live for the attention and love they receive from a child. I have heard misinformed people state that this breed is strictly for adults. These dogs are full of energy and can certainly keep up with kids. They are eager to play and get into any trouble they might find, although keep in mind that they have a mind of their own, and this feisty dog will not do anything is doesn't want to do. Doxies are a wonderful family pet, as long as they are treated properly. There is nothing like the love between a child and a dog that is a bond that certainly will grow over the years, as the two grow up together.

If you have children, I would suggest setting some ground rules before bringing your adorable little puppy home. Children naturally want to pick up and hold their puppy, while there is nothing wrong with this, too much holding is no good, especially if the puppy doesn't feel completely secure in their arms. Everyone should be taught how to properly pick up, hold, and set down the puppy gently. It is best to do this while the child is sitting down, and can place the puppy comfortably on his lap. Make sure that each child learns how to do this, so that the puppy is safe and secure. With very young children, I strongly discourage them picking up the puppy at all because this breed needs to be held properly with back support, therefore younger children should only handle them when sitting down on the floor. Doxies are known to be very squirmy, and dropping them, can result in major injury, especially to their long backs. I suggest that the children sit on the floor and play with the puppy on its own level, and allow the puppy to jump on and off of their laps, to not only avoid unnecessary handling, but the possibility of dropping the puppy from a standing position. Once a Dachshund injuries its back, it will never fully recover, and you can expect vet visits for the problem.

The more, good, social experiences that Dachshund puppies get, especially with children and other pets the better, just make sure that you always supervise constantly to avoid problems in the early stages.

Children should also be taught to leave the puppy alone while it is eating. Dogs can sometimes bite when they feel their food is being threatened; however a Doxie biting over food is a rare thing. Even though the threat of a bite is low, the puppy will eat better, and digest his food easier when it is allowed quiet time to eat, without any distractions. Children also need to understand that feeding the puppy is best left to the adults of the house, as certain food items can be toxic. Children like to share what they are eating, especially with a beloved pet, so this must be discussed with your child.

As a family you should discuss and work out schedules for who will be the responsible party taking the puppy out, especially when it's being potty trained, and who will feed and check on its water.

Children need to be taught that although dogs can't speak, they experience pain, hunger, fear, loneliness, hurt and other emotions that humans feel. Children should be taught to NEVER pull the dog's hair, ears, or tail. Always keep close supervision with your children and your Doxie. As your child grows and matures, so will your dog, and the two will create special memories of times spent together.

Dachshund's will usually get along very well with children especially if your children know how to treat the dog kindly, the dachshund has a good temperament because it came from a good breeding pool, and your Doxie puppy has been raised with children.

The Dachshund Puppy and Other Pets

If you already have another dog in the home, obviously there will be a time of transition for both the existing pet and the new Dachshund puppy. The key is to make the first introduction to each other slowly. When you first bring the new puppy home, it is best to have the existing pet in a cage, on a leash or have another adult hold it tightly. After about 15 minutes, bring the current pet out, and hold the new puppy, allowing them to smell each other and investigate what the other one is about.

During this time, you must pay close attention to your current pet for signs of jealously. To insure that this isn't going to be a problem, give extra attention to your existing pet to help it make the adjustment, do not make the mistake of giving the new puppy all of the attention. This is a common understandable mistake, because the new puppy is fresh and exciting, but you don't want to make your other pet feel that it is being pushed to the side as old news.

There is always the chance that your pets will not like each other. Sometimes the existing pet will view the new puppy as a threat. You may hear a few growls exchanged, and they will naturally determine the pecking order between them. If your existing pet is large, you will have to intervene quickly, the larger pet needs to understand that it could injure a tiny Doxie. The larger dog must be extremely gentle and not get overly excited even during play as not to pounce on your small Doxie, which could result in a back injury, even though the larger dog didn't mean to injure your Doxie, it can happen accidently. Obviously dogs, closer in size are best and safest together. As a word of warning, you should realize that Dachshunds can have a tendency to become jealous, yet will do well with another toy breed in the home as long as the other dog isn't snippy. A Dachshund will especially enjoy the company of another wiener dog. If you know that you want to have two Dachshunds and can financially afford it, I highly recommend buying two from the same litter, and raising them together.

It is important that until your older pet and new puppy completely get along that they be supervised at all times when placed together. Until you are 100% certain, do not feel bad about keeping them in separate rooms, cages, or placing the new puppy safely in a playpen, so that the older pet can sniff, and see it, but not injure it. Always reassure your existing pet by giving them extra attention and love, and talk to your older pet while handling the new puppy, so it doesn't feel unwanted and no longer loved by the family.

Both pets should have their own food and water dishes, sharing can sometimes cause problems. I have owned as many as seven dogs at one time; all had the full run of the household. I never had one problem when introducing a new addition or puppy into the pack. I can tell you from my experience, that dogs seem to know and understand their own breed, and are usually happy to have each other for company. When placing different breeds together, it can be a little trickier, so you must use caution, care, common sense and most of all supervise.

In my own experience, many of the smaller breeds just don't usually get along with cats, and I would use much caution when attempting to put the two together, and I really can't say that I could even recommend trying it.

I have a caged parrot, and my dogs seem to tolerate it's talking, but I know that if they had the opportunity to get a hold of it while it was out of the cage, it would be a disaster. I only remove my parrot from the cage when my dogs are outside or locked in another room. Remember that a Dachshund hound has natural hunting instincts which can and will take over. Expect your Doxie to chase and bark at any squirrel that has evaded its territory, such as the backyard. If you verbally scold your puppy for this behavior from the beginning it will curb it from becoming a constant barking problem, and the dog will come to understand that you will not tolerate the barking, and learn to ignore the squirrels as being something you deem acceptable visitors in the yard.

Potty Training Your Dachshund Hound

Different breeds have different levels of learning. Some breeds are very easy to train while others are very difficult. I'm not going to lie to you, Doxies are one of the hardest breeds to housebreak, especially males. The reason males seem to be even harder to train than females is due to their natural instinct to mark their territory. If you have an unsprayed female dog in the house, and bring in an unaltered male, you can expect him to be even harder to train.

Successful housebreaking takes a lot of patience. A crate serves several purposes and it is by far the easiest way to housebreak your new Dachshund. Dogs are den animals and are usually very happy and secure to go into their own crate, so that they can rest undisturbed. They will not want to relieve themselves in their own crate because it is a limited area, which is why most owners will choose to crate train their dogs. The crate itself should contain a bed, such as a soft fleece baby blanket, and it should be large enough for your dog to turn around in. Do not feed or water your Doxie while it is in the crate. The crate is for short-term stays like a trip in the car, or while you go out to the store for an hour or so, or when you simply do not have the time to monitor your little puppy. Please do not make the mistake of thinking that you can keep your Dachshund in a crate while you go to work all day, because that is unreasonably cruel.

You must think of the using the crate as you would a playpen for a child when you cannot directly watch their every move. The crate will keep your Dachshund from injuring itself or causing any destructive chewing on furniture or other household items.

Keep in mind that the crate should not be used as punishment, because the puppy will not understand that concept. The crate offers you the opportunity to praise your Doxie for being good, instead of scolding it for the mess that they made for you while you were gone.

Responding afterwards to your Doxies accident makes for bad housebreaking experience for the both of you, and it can also make your dog fear you. Never hit or punish a Doxie to housebreak it, the dog doesn't truly understand what they are being punished for. Just like small children, a Doxie will learn faster if it is a pleasant experience, and will not do well if all you do is yell at it. Positive training methods achieve faster results.

You must be consistent and pay attention to what your puppy is doing. If you do not have the time to watch your Doxie then crate the puppy. Before crating it just make sure your Doxie goes outside and remember when you remove your puppy from the crate to take the puppy outside immediately, and praise it when it goes potty.

If you are training your Doxie to go outside, the more accidents you have inside the longer it will take to train. Never give a new puppy full run of the house until it is completely housebroken, because that makes it impossible for you to watch it, and react to an accident.

You should take your Doxie outside as soon as it wakes up in the morning, or immediately from a nap, after it eats, after you play with them, and before they go to bed or place it back into their crate. Naturally they should go out every couple of hours during the day.

Make sure that you are consistent with your method. The best secret to housebreaking any dog is to watch your dog all the time. If you can keep your dog from having accidents in the house, and catching them, you can get them outside in time, to reinforce that is the place they should go.

Never push their nose in an accident, it is a natural for them to go potty, and they do not understand why you are doing that to them, and you could make your dog afraid to go to the bathroom. I believe this is a common potty training mistake that causes some dogs to eat their own stool, to hide what they have done. As a note, I should also tell you that some dogs will also eat their own stool due to poor nutrition; therefore it is important that you feed them the proper diet, which I will discuss later in the book.

Potty training should begin the day you bring your puppy home. Pick a spot in your yard that you want your Doxie to use as its potty area. Place your puppy in this area and tell it to "go potty" or some other word you would like to use (remember always use the same word, be consistent). Keep repeating the word till your Doxie goes potty, and then praise your puppy. You can also give a special reward like a small treat that they only get when they go potty outside. I give my puppies a piece of cheerios cereal for a special reward and they love it. If you do not wait for your Doxie to go potty, he or she will go as soon as they get in the house, which is not your objective. Always, always praise your puppy for doing a good job and they will do it again on command when they hear the words "go potty". You will spend a lot of time in the first couple of days waiting and hoping for the big moment; just remember if he/she does not do it outside they will do it inside. If you see your dog going potty in the house, the key word here is "see", because this is not the same as finding potty in your house and knowing that your dog is the only one who could have done it. If the latter is the case, just clean it up and do nothing to the dog. If you catch your Doxie in the act, move quickly, pick your puppy up and take it to its potty place. Use the phrase "go potty" or use your own phrase. Once it finishes going, then praise your Doxie. Praising your Doxie is the most important part, as your pet wants to please you. Giving the puppy a treat will speed up the process too. Do not rush your Doxie when potty training, it may be cold or rainy or you may be tired, if you make this a bad experience for your Doxie it will take considerably longer to house train. Remember puppies can tell if you are happy with them or not by how you speak and treat them. If you take your Doxie out at night and it will not defecate but as soon as you bring it back in the house the dog defecates, you know your dog did have to go but you did not wait long enough for them to do their business. Make sure you give your Doxie enough time to go and do not play with the puppy at this time or let it play with anything while you are waiting for them to go potty. This is business, not playtime, and the dog will come to understand the difference.

Another method of housebreaking is to use a training pad/wee-wee pad/pee pad. Many owners of toy breeds prefer this method. You can purchase these at any local pet store or online. Look for the pads that are treated, they will attract your puppy to go on the pads. This is a very easy method if you are using an old child's playpen, by putting a blanket on one side along with food and water, and the training pad on the other side of the pen, creating two separate areas. When the dog wakes up, after every meal, after playtime, and generally every 2 or 3 hours, place the puppy on the pad, and tell it to go potty. You want to re-enforce this, and praise after the puppy goes. Then you can eventually move the pad to a place of your liking and your dog will continue to use it. If you decide to use puppy-training pads, you won't have to worry about letting your dog go outside, which is especially nice if you live in a harsh weather climate.

Showing Your Dachshund Hound

No matter what you have heard, dog shows are complicated and tend to be quite political. If you know that you want to enter this world, do yourself a favor and purchase your puppy from someone that lives, eats, and breeds for showing. They will be your best guide to the dog shows, and will be more than willing to help you learn the ropes, especially since you will be showing a dog that they whelped.

To get started in the show world, join a local kennel club, either an all breed club or a Dachshund Hound club, or if it's possible join both. Your breeder should be able to give you this information on where to find these clubs locally or you can always call the AKC.

A local club can provide you with all the information you need on training classes for the show ring, and also classes for obedience and agility classes if you are interested. These classes are informative, but of course the best way to learn and get practice for the show ring, is to attend dog shows and watch, that will also give you a better understanding of what the judges and the competitors do at these shows. These clubs also offer professional dog handlers that you can hire to show your dog, while you relax and enjoy viewing the competition from a ringside seat.

When entering a show, you will be required to know all the rules. You can purchase and order a copy of the official rulebook from the AKC. Read it, re-read it, and if possible put it to memory. Understand that because you are new to the show ring, doesn't mean that you will be forgiven for breaking rules, in fact the masters will be more than willing to point out your mistakes.

Showing your dog is a thrill like no other, and the competition is rewarding. First you need to understand the different types of dog shows. First we will discuss the conformation events, the dog's overall appearance and structure, which are purely intended to evaluate the breeding stock, another induction of the dog's ability to produce quality puppies. A few simple rules to know about this type of dog show. Your dog must be registered with the AKC, has to be 6 months of age or older, and cannot be spayed or neutered.

There are three kinds of conformation dog shows, All-breed shows, Specialty shows, and Group shows. The All-breed shows have competitions for as many as 150 breeds, which you will usually see on television. The Specialty shows (a great place to start) are for a specific kind of breed, such as Dachshund Hounds. The Group shows are for the seven groups, in the case of a Doxie, you would be entering in the Hound Group.

In each of these kinds of shows, the judges will examine each dog, and then present awards to the dogs that are the closest to the breed's official standard. They are looking not only at appearance, but also temperament and movement. The judges will check each dog using their hands, in order to make sure that the teeth, muscles, coat, and bones all conform to the breed standard. They will watch each dog standing in profile for overall balance, and then study the gait (walk) of your dog. Many dogs that are in competition at the conformation shows are really competing for points toward their dogs AKC championships. A dog must earn 15 points; including two majors (which are wins of three, four or five points) that have been awarded by at least three different judges, to gain the title of "AKC Champion of Record." The amount of championship points that are awarded at a dog show totally depends on the amount of males or females entered into that breed of competition on that day. Obviously, the more entries, the greater amount of points a dog can win, with the maximum number of points awarded being 5 points. Males and female dogs always compete separately within their breed and there are seven classes of competition that are offered.

The Puppy Class, which is for dogs between six to twelve months old, which have not yet received their champions.

The Twelve to Eighteen Months Class, for dogs of that age that still hasn't received their champions.

The Novice Class, which is for dogs six months of age or older, which haven't won any points towards their championship, or won three first prizes in the Novice Class.

The Amateur Owner Handler Class, for dogs that are at least six months of age that haven't earned their championship. As the name would suggest the dog must be handled by its official registered owner. The owner must not be a professional dog handler, AKC approved judge or an employee of a professional handler.

The Bred By Exhibitor Class is for dogs that are shown by their owner and breeder, and are not yet champions.

The American Bred Class, is for dogs that were bred and born in the U.S. and haven't earned their championship yet.

The Open Class is for any dog that is at least 6 months of age.

When the judges have completed scoring all of the above classes, and the dogs have been awarded first place in each class, they will compete again to see who is the best of the best. Once again, males and females are judged separately, and awarded "Winners Dog" for the male, and "Winners Bitch" for the female, and each will receive championship points. Those two dogs will then compete with the champions for the Best of Breed Award.

The way dog shows work is by using the process of elimination, until the last dog standing receives the Best in Show award. Only the Best of Breed Dachshund Hound winner can advance to the group competition of Hound Group. Then the Hound Group winner will compete against the other Best of the Group winners, which are Sporting, Toy, Working, Terrier, Non-Sporting and Herding, for the coveted title of Best in Show.

There are other events at dog shows, which can also be a lot of fun and a great way for you to train and bond with your Dachshund Hound. The Agility Show, features dogs running through an obstacle course, and they are judged on how fast they complete the course. Naturally courses are set up different at each of the events and will feature balance beam, teeter-totter, and hoops to jump through.

You can also place your Doxie in the Obedience Event, which will give you the opportunity to show how well your dog has been trained. You give your dog commands, and will be judged on how well your Dachshund Hound listens to you.

As a note, the AKC also offers something called Junior Showmanship Class. This is for children between the ages of 9 to 18, and they are judged on how they present their dogs to the judges.

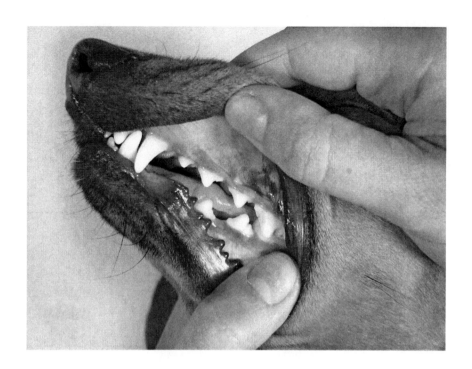

Dachshund Hound Teeth

Doxies are known to have problems with their teeth throughout their entire lives, if they aren't cared for properly. A puppy will start to get baby teeth around 4 weeks of age, and will have 28 puppy teeth.

Around 4 to 6 months of age, your puppy will begin losing puppy teeth, and their permanent teeth will start to come in. Generally, you will see the incisor teeth around 4 months, the canine teeth around 5 months, an after 6 months the molars. By 10 months old, your Dachshund Hound should have all 42 permanent adult teeth. You must remember that these are purely guidelines, as each child is different; the same goes for each puppy. As a general rule, the smaller the puppy, the longer it will take for the teeth to come in. You will want to keep a close eye on your puppy's teeth, because Doxies are famous for having problems during this time. It is not uncommon for Doxies puppy teeth to remain, requiring them to be removed by a veterinarian. In many cases you will see the adult teeth growing behind the puppy teeth. If this is the case, the sooner you take your puppy to the vet and have them removed the better, as this will have an effect on the placement of their permanent adult teeth.

During the time of teething you can do several things to ease the pain and control your puppies chewing.

Make chicken soup (either homemade without salt or store bought low sodium) ice cubes. Your puppy will enjoy the taste, and be happy to chew on them. Fill the ice cube trays only half full, so that your tiny puppy can get these cubes in their mouth. This will numb pain, and help loosen the baby teeth, and also help the adult teeth cut thru the gums. You can soak a rag in water, wring it out, and then pop it into the freeze, and give it to your puppy to chew on as a toy. Always discourage your puppy from biting on your arm or hand. This can become a habit, and when the teething stage is done, a puppy who was allowed to chew on you, may continue to bite and chew. Make sure that you scold your Dachshund, so that it understands biting on you is causing you pain. Then replace your hand with an object, toy, rag or ice cube to gnaw on. Remember to have patience with your puppy, because it will be experiencing pain and discomfort, and don't be surprised to see some bleeding gums. Your puppy will want to chew more during this time. There are several dog toys on the market especially designed for a teething puppy, which are made to go into a freezer, this is a small price to pay, especially if it saves shoes or furniture. It is rare to find puppy teeth, as they typically swallow them.

Good Oral hygiene is important for a Dachshund Hound, and must be practiced from the beginning. You can start cleaning your puppy's teeth with a wet cloth and then graduate to a soft dog toothbrush or you can purchase a soft child sizes toothbrush. Most puppies won't like this at first, but the earlier you introduce this, the easier it will get. I recommend that you brush your dog's teeth at least several times a week, using dog toothpaste, which can be purchased at most pet stores or online. Please note that you can't use human toothpaste on your dog.

Doxies have early tooth decay problems, it's in their breeding, but there are some things you can do to help. Have your dog's teeth professionally cleaned by your Veterinarian at least once a year. This is a painless procedure, as the vet will place your dog under general anesthesia, and it's also not nearly as expensive as you would think. I have known some vets to even recommend antibacterial treatments before tooth infections happen.

Good dental care is important for your dog's health. Poor dental hygiene can lead to pain for your pet and foul smelling breathe caused by the tooth decay. Taking good care of your dog's teeth does not take a lot of time or effort. It's very sad to see a senior Dachshund Hound with only a few teeth left in its mouth, struggling to chew food. I also recommend dental chew toys to help remove tartar build-up, which is a huge problem for this breed. I don't believe in giving Doxies bones or rawhide chews. Bones can cause the teeth to shatter and break and the dogs usually end up eating the rawhide chews. There are several other prospective problems with rawhide or pig ears. First the obvious that it is a choking hazard especially for a puppy as pieces can and will break off as they chew it. Second, the rawhide can cause major stomach irritation in smaller breeds, or even a severe gastric disorder from ingesting it. Please understand that due to the fact that manufacturing of rawhide dog chews and bones is completely unregulated, you have no control as to how safe it is for your pet. There have been many reports of salmonella causing dogs to get sick, and in addition to that, dangerous chemicals have been found during the processing of them.

Dental problems can cause many other health problems that include kidney failure, heart problems, and sinus and eye infections.

Teeth are also a result of the food you are feeding your dog. Your dog's teeth will not clean themselves because they are chewing kibble dog food. That is a statement the dog food companies want you to believe, you can't clean teeth by scraping them with food, they must be brushed with toothpaste. I'm not a believer in dog food at all, not kibble, moist, semi-moist or canned, but more about that later in this book.

Dachshund Hound Ears

Every dog breed has a different size or shape to their ears, and each seems to have some kind of problem that comes along with it. Dachshunds have the long, floppy ears, that just seem to be extremely susceptible to ear infections.

You do want to keep an eye on your dog's ears for excessive waxy buildup, redness or inflammation around the ear, retention of dirt, any foreign materials or objects in the ear canal. It is also a good idea to actually smell your dog's ears, because a foul odor is often a sign of an ear infection. Keep in mind that mites, fleas, and ticks like the dark and somewhat moist inaccessible area of the ear. If you think that your dog has a problem, consult with your veterinarian as soon as possible. In the case of a severe infection, neglecting it could result in deafness. Other telltale signs that your Doxie is suffering from an ear problem are, excessive shaking of its head, pawing and scratching at the ears. Should you also notice your dog has a tilted head; this can be a sign that the side, which is being held down, is the painful side. Your Dachshund Hound can't speak to you, but they do have other ways of communicating, pay attention to your dog for clues of illness.

To lower your Doxie's chance of getting an ear infection, you should clean the ears out once a month and keep them dry. There are many different ideas when it comes to Dachshund Hound ear cleaning solutions, but I feel good ones can be made at home using several different ingredients you probably already own. Below I will list several different solutions. If your dog's ear infection seems to persist for longer than a week, even after you've used cleaning solutions on it, you should see a veterinarian.

If you have the long hair or wire hair Doxie and take it to the groomers routinely, they rarely if ever will get an ear infection, because the groomer will do a good cleaning, although they are still prone to getting wax buildup inside of the ear. If you are grooming your dog at home, only a gentle cleaning should be needed. Never poke or probe the internal ear canal, do not use cotton tipped swab. These only push dirt deeper into the ear canal, causing a serious problem. For a gentle cleaning, you can use mineral oil applied to a cotton ball, and lightly wipe the surface of the external ear. Below are a few other homemade cleaning solutions which can be made for ears that just seem to need extra care.

Alcohol and Vinegar Cleaning:
1/3 cup rubbing alcohol
1/3 cup white vinegar
1/3 cup water

Mix ingredients together and place into a dropper. Generously flush infected ear , and let solution sit while holding the dogs head to one side for 2 to 3 minutes, and then drain solution from ear, by tilting head.. The alcohol dries out the ear, and the vinegar kills any bacteria that might be residing therein.

Alcohol and Boric Acid Cleaning:
16 oz. bottle rubbing alcohol
4 Tbsp. Boric Acid Powder

Add the boric acid powder to the bottle of rubbing alcohol and shake well. Apply this solution to your Doxie's ears twice a day using an eye dropper and then following up with massaging, so that the drops go into the ear canal. Wipe the excessive with a clean tissue. The alcohol will dry out the ear, and the boric acid will soothe any of the burning. This is a stronger solution, and it can be cut down using some water.

Dachshund Bathing, Brushing, Nails and Grooming

As far as bathing, brushing and grooming, a Dachshund Hound is one of the easiest breeds to care for. All three of the coats are considered to be light shedders and this breed does not suffer from any problems with having a strong odor. Each coat has different requirements for brushing and grooming.

Always use a good quality specially formulated dog shampoo and conditioner if your Doxie's coat requires it. Make sure you are using the correct brush that matches your particular dogs coat type.

Bathing

Most people make the mistake of bathing their dogs too often. Naturally we all love the smell of a freshly pampered dog coming back from the groomers or even after we have given them a bath ourselves, but bathing too much can cause problems. A bath will make your Doxie's coat softer and smoother, but this happens because giving them a bath removes their fat hair, which Dachshunds produce. The fat hair is an insulating layer that helps to protect the dog from natural elements. I don't recommend that you give your dog a bath more than every 60 days. When doing it yourself at home, be extra careful not to get water, shampoo or conditioner into the ears or eyes, and always make sure when drying that you gently towel dry the inside of the ears. Be careful that you rinse all the shampoo and conditioner out; otherwise it will cause skin irritations. Rub the fur dry with a soft clean towel, or if you wish, you can use a blow dryer on a low setting.

Brushing

Smooth Dachshund: This coat requires the least amount of grooming. Only use a soft brush, no wire brushes on this coat, or a hard rubber brush or mitt. A great brush for this coat type is a tiny baby brush that you would use on a newborn child. Grooming mitts are also good for this shorthaired breed and can add polish and shine to the coat.

This coat can also be wiped down using a cloth or baby wipes. Since some may have very thin coats, and almost appear to even have balding spots care must be given when out in the sun, as they can burn their skin with too much exposure.

Long Haired Dachshund: This coat should be brushed and combed daily, especially since the longer hair can tend to get dirty. Use a good quality pet brush and metal dog comb. This coat can mat, therefore it is easier to brush and comb when you section off the hair and work only one area at a time. Pay extra attention to areas behind ears and where the hair is the longest as those are the area's most likely to mat. In the case of a severe knot or matting, you can either cut out the knot or use a spray on detangler and gently comb it out. Brush through each section, and then follow with a comb. If the comb hits a tangle, go back over it with the brush. Remember that using a spray on detangler can help smooth out minor tangles but won't fix major matting. When major tangles are encountered, hold the matt of hair as close to the skin as possible so the hairs are not pulling up from the skin. Once you can comb through the section without hitting any tangles, move on to the next section. This coat should be blow dried after a bath.

Wire Haired Dachshund: This coat should be brushed using a wire bristle dog brush, and metal comb. This coat should be cut and trimmed about twice a year for good maintenance, and may need to be stripped, which I recommend being done by a professional dog groomer. A good daily brushing will remove loose hair, and therefore you will have less noticeable shedding in your home. As a note, adding omega fish oil into your Doxie's diet, will improve the hair coat and shine coat quality.

I like to brush my dogs in the evening while I'm watching television, just placing one on my lap at a time. If you give your Doxie attention, and talk to it while brushing, it will come to enjoy this attention. You will want to start this ritual immediately when you bring your puppy home, so that it comes to understand this is a positive thing. Take your time, especially if your Doxie has tangles and mats, so that you avoid causing any pain. If you brush daily, this shouldn't be a problem.

Always brush the coat in the direction of the hair growth, starting at the head and working towards the tail and down the legs. Don't forget to brush the underneath of the body, and the pit areas of the upper legs.

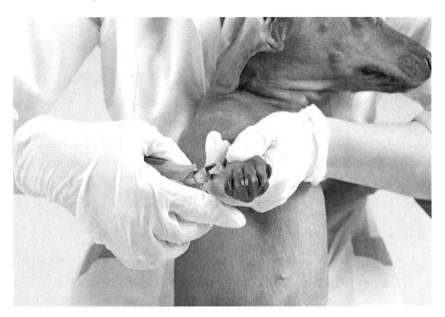

Nail Care

Some Doxies will not need their nails trimmed, as this happens naturally from exercising on pavement during regular walks. If you notice that your Dachshunds nails are longer than they should be, then it is time to trim them. If your Doxie isn't wearing down its own nails and you have to cut them, make sure that you do so frequently, so you won't have to cut much off, just having to snip the tips. Some dogs have a fear of getting their nails clipped, so the sooner it is done during the puppy stage, the better off, as with time, they will get used to it. Buy a good quality trimmer that is made just for dogs, so you don't risk splitting or cracking the nails during cutting. Extra care must be given because you have to avoid cutting the quick, which contains nerves and blood vessels. If this quick is accidentally cut, the nail will breed, usually quite a lot, requiring a styptic powder to stop it, so don't ever trim your dog's nails without first having this on hand. If you are afraid to cut your dogs nail, most groomers will be more than happy to do just this service for you, for a very small fee. If you are planning on doing this yourself, ask your vet or groomer to show you how to do this the first time, and then try it yourself while they watch you. If your Dachshund is on a regular schedule with a professional groomer, you will not have to worry about nail care, as the groomer will automatically trim them.

<u>Grooming</u>

Most long hair and wire hair Doxie owners will take their dogs to a professional groomer. A long hair should go 3 or 4 times a year, and a wire hair twice a year. A groomer will give your Doxie a bath, trim the nails, trim the hair on the ears, around the anus, between the pads of the paws, and in some cases around the eyes. A groomer should express your dog's anal glands, which is one of the unpleasant aspects of being a dog groomer. The reason dogs have these glands are, when a dog passes a stool, pressure is placed on the glands which are located on either side of the anus, and these glands secrete a fluid along with the stool. Every dog has a different odor to their secretion in order to identify him, which is one of the reasons dogs will sniff each other's behinds. On rare occasions, a dog's anal glands will become impacted, and Doxies are one of the breeds that can have this problem. The signs of impacted anal glands are, dragging their butt on the floor often called scooting, tail chasing, swollen anus, and excessive licking or biting of the tail or anus area.

The sooner your puppy goes to the groomer the better they will be about it. Make sure you locate a good groomer, make phone calls, and don't be afraid to ask them questions. The shop should be clean, and you should be able to see them working on dogs when you enter. If they have something to hide, and you aren't able to view the working area, which is in the back for employees only, take your dog and leave. Make sure the groomer that will be handling your Dachshund will do so gently, and carefully. If you have the opportunity to observe them working on a dog, watch their manner, and see if they talk and reassure the dog they are working on.

You need to take several things into consideration before trusting your Dachshund Hound with a complete stranger. Grooming is often a stressful time for your dog, so finding the correct groomer will be helpful, and your dog will develop a relationship with them.

The best way to find a good groomer is to ask around at the dog clubs or shows. Another option is to check with the dog groomer associations; because if a groomer is a member you have a better chance that he is reputable. Make sure that the groomer has the proper certification in your state and is licensed. Some groomers do certain breeds better than others, look for someone that has a large Doxie clientele base. If you aren't happy with the first haircut, find someone else; it may take you several groomers before you find the right one. You can expect your dog will be in their care for several hours, but when you pick them up, you'll receive a fresh smelling, happy dog, and one that is happy to see their owner has returned.

Praise your dog when you return home with it. I tell my dogs how pretty they look and make a big fuss over them remember Doxies love attention. If you make going to the groomer a happy, positive, rewarding time for your dog, it will be eager to get into the car and go the next time.

Try to set up a regular schedule and stick to it as best you can. Grooming is an important part of your dogs well being. If you decide that you want to do all of your dog's grooming yourself, than you should observe this breed being groomed several times before you make the attempt.

Immunizations

I'm listing here a basic immunization schedule; however, many vets follow their own, depending on your location, and your Dachshund Hounds need, because certain diseases are a greater risk in some areas than in others.

The most common puppy immunization schedule covers the most essential shots. Your puppy will need 3 sets of vaccinations including one rabies shot to be protected for the first year of life. Then you can follow with annual boosters, however, be careful that you don't over-vaccinate, you must keep careful records. At least one or two of these shots should have been done by the breeders vet before the purchase, make sure you have the paperwork on those when you pick up your puppy, so that you don't duplicate these shots.

Puppy Shots

6 – 8 weeks	DHLPP & Corona
11-12 weeks	DHLPP & Corona
15-16 weeks	DHLPP & Corona
16 weeks	Rabies

The DHLPP shot is a combination that covers, distemper, hepatitis, leptospirosis, parainfluenza, bordetella and parvovirus.

Distemper... an airborne viral disease of the lungs, intestines and brain
Hepatitis... a viral disease of the liver
Leptospirosis... a bacterial disease of the urinary tract
Parainfluenza... infectious bronchitis
Parvovirus... a viral disease of the intestines
Rabies... a viral disease fatal to humans and other animals

Bordetella Bronchiseptica is a bacterial agent that causes the respiratory disease, kennel cough.

Corona… a viral disease of the intestines

Adult Dogs (after 1 year)

DHLPP… Yearly
Rabies… Every three years (after 2nd shot)
Bordetella

Remember that vaccinations for your Doxie's health are the best kind of medicine because prevention is easier and better than the cure to these diseases. Many of these diseases can be fatal so it is imperative that you follow a vaccination program carefully. There are other vaccinations available for prevention of Lyme disease which you should discuss with your vet, depending on the risk assessment of your area. You should address any concerns or questions about these shots with your vet. The only mandatory vaccination in the United States for dogs is the rabies one, but I believe that it is a foolish risk to take, not to do the others. Some breeds do have side effects from their shots, which include things like a fever or swelling in the area of the injection, but Dachshund Hounds usually do very well.

In case you are wondering how vaccinations work they mimic the process of the disease. A weakened form of the virus is injected into the body, and the immune system is triggered into producing antibodies to protect the body against the disease. The body then remembers the virus and will respond to any future exposure to it and finally more appropriate antibodies get produced. Puppies are especially at risk from various diseases as their immunity is so low. Puppies receive immunity from certain diseases from their mother before weaning, if she has been vaccinated. After weaning, when puppies are eating on their own they need to be vaccinated as soon as possible. Canine Parvovirus is particularly deadly to young puppies. The above info on creating a Dog Vaccination Plan and schedule with a Veterinary Surgeon will help to ensure the safety of your puppy. It is essential that you be provided with a vaccination history when you purchase a puppy. It is common for puppies to have worms so a basic wormer for Roundworms and Hookworms is recommended with the first vaccinations. I would expect that your breeder has already had the puppy de-wormed at least once.

Pet Health Insurance

Most pet health insurance policies typically do not cover routine health care, examinations and vaccinations, but this also serves the purpose of keeping premiums very low. Pet health insurance is generally used for catastrophic, expensive and unexpected events. Advanced and emergency veterinary care can be very expensive. Pets with serious injuries or illness are commonly put down because of lack of funds to save them, but with this insurance you will never have to worry about, that heartbreaking decision. The advancement of veterinary medicine has largely kept pace with human medicine, however, so has the costs. As a pet owner, you now have more options, and treatment plans available, such as cardiac surgery, MRI, CT and ultrasound imaging.

Dogs are living longer than they have in the past because many fatal diseases such as distemper have been virtually eliminated with vaccinations. Adding more years to your pet's life is great, but you need to plan for the conditions that old age presents. You can better help your

Dachshund Hound, and make informed decisions about its health when you aren't stressing out over the cost of the bill.

Make sure that you research and shop around for your pet health insurance policy. You will want to look for a company that issues reimbursement based on the actual vet bill. Many pet insurance companies utilize outdated benefit schedules; that haven't kept up with the cost of living, so make sure you know what you are getting for your money. Read all the fine print, so that it is clear about what is covered and what is not. There are several plans on the market that will allow you to sleep better at night knowing that should some unfortunate accident or illness strike your Doxie, it will not create a financial burden on you, and you'll be able to do everything you can to save your precious pet. Many vets' offices have pamphlets available for different plans, and can usually offer you helpful information about which company you should choose, based on their patients experiences with them.

I know that many people in the United States don't have health insurance for themselves, so the very thought of having it for their pet may seem crazy, however, the rates on these policies are usually so cheap, that you will not want to pass it up.

Dachshund Hound Health Concerns

Overall a well-bred Dachshund Hound is typically a very healthy, hearty dog. This breed has a long life expectancy of approximately 10 to 12 years. This chapter is not meant to scare you, but you should make yourself familiar with the health problems that are associated with this breed and learn to recognize the warning signs and symptoms. I know that at first glance the following list of potential health problems is long; however, I could make a list as long with any other breed, because each breed has a list of problems that commonly affect them. I would rather give you all the information than to leave some of it out, even though you will hopefully never need this information, I think that it is best you are aware of it, so that you can look for these problems. There isn't data on the percentage of Doxies with the following ailments, and I'm not suggesting that all Dachshund Hounds have these ailments. The Doxies problem conditions can be inherited, congenital or acquired. If we continue research and good selective breeding practices most of these conditions will become things of the past, the breed will become stronger, and perhaps live longer. There is much currently happening in the world of research, especially when it comes to DNA mapping, and I hope that someday, we will be able to test each Doxie being bred, in order to assure that each puppy it produces will be healthy and happy.

All breeds seem to suffer from one condition or another, as dogs are living breathing beings, therefore disease or illness can strike them at any time, just like a human. Dachshund Hounds are lively by nature, so you will easily be able to notice when your Doxie is sick or experiencing pain or discomfort, because the dog will automatically be less active. It is important that you contact your vet if you have any doubts about your pet's health, as hesitation can be fatal. Naturally regular vet checkups play an important part in your dog's health.

Intervertebral Disc Disease

A disc that is not functioning properly which causes pain, problems walking, stumbling, severe neck pain, and even paralysis. This is a major neurologic problem for this breed. Treatments can go from non-invasive doses of anti-inflammatory steroids, muscle relaxants and bed rest and in the worst case surgery. In addition, alternative treatment methods including chiropractic manipulations, acupuncture can be tried. The intervertebral disk consists of two regions: the outer layer called *annulus fibrosus* of cartilage-like material and the central region called *nucleus pulposus*. The central region is a gel-like structure in the young animal which becomes progressively dehydrated and less gel-like with age. The exact cause of the degenerative process is not yet fully understood, but is commonly attributed to influence of genetic, hormonal, autoimmune (immune system disorder), and mechanical factors. The Dachshund is especially prone to broken backs, spinal and disc problems due to the dog's length. You must be careful not to injure the back or allow things to fall on the back of a Dachshund as severe spinal damage can be a death sentence.

The long, low to the ground body of the Dachshund can in itself become a contributing factor to the health issues that can develop in the breed. It is important to avoid over feeding the Dachshund as additional weight on the long spinal cord leads to increasing likelihood of paralysis and movement and mobility problems as the dog ages. In addition there are also some genetic factors involved in the development of mobility problems within the breed. It is essential for owners to understand that even following all the recommended management and exercise issues for the breed there is still a chance that genetic factors may cause temporary or permanent loss of movement in the hind quarters for even a healthy, slender Dachshund.

One key factor that owners need to consider is to avoid any type of jumping activities for a Dachshund. Jumping up and down off of furniture or beds puts huge pressure on the middle of the back, leading to a greater risk of disc problems. Another essential preventative measure is to keep the dog lean and well exercised as this helps the body, legs and spine stay strong while avoiding the additional pressure that weight puts on the spine.

Pannus

A disorder of the cornea of the eye usually showing up in the 4 to 7 year range with an increase in dogs living at higher elevations. Initially, redness, ocular discharge and brown pigment may be seen in the conjunctiva (white tissue of the eye). White infiltrates made up of inflammatory cells then invade the clear cornea. Next blood vessels invade the cornea. Finally pink connective tissue grows into the cornea and later becomes brown. In a small number of cases, two other symptoms may occur either alone or together. A thickening, redness, loss of pigmentation and lumpiness of the third eyelid may occur. This is called a plasmoma. The other condition which may occur is chronic, erosive ulceration of the lower eyelid near the inner and outer corners of the eye. Pannus is uncomfortable to the dog. When treated adequately, your pet can be free of this irritation even though the corneas may not clear up completely. Despite intensive research efforts, no permanent cure exists for pannus. However, in the vast majority of cases, the disease progress can be halted and the problem kept stable. This seems to be more of a problem in dapples.

Entropion

Eye irritation caused by the eyelids and lashes rolling inward. The problem is usually inherited and found in young, adult dogs. It can come from an eyelid spasm. Affected eyes will be held partially shut and tear excessively. Both eyes will usually be affected the same. Treatment for the condition requires eye surgery. Entropion most often affects the outer aspect of the lower eyelids of one or both eyes. The upper eyelids may also be involved. In some dogs the entire eyelid is rolled inward, or a portion of the lid may be rolled in and another portion is rolled out. Look for eye tearing, squinting, inability to see well, dog pawing at eyes, thick discharge from eyes, and rolling of the eyelid, including wetness on the hair adjacent to eyelids.

Distichiasis

An eye condition involving the cornea. Eyelashes, growing improperly on the inner surface of the eyelid cause corneal ulcers due to the constant rubbing and irritation. The problem is fixed by having the vet remove the lashes if the ulcers don't heal. This seems to be more of a problem in dapples.

Progressive Retinal Atrophy

This is an inherited, untreatable disease of the retina affecting both eyes causing blindness. It's in the genes of the dog and is not painful. Starts with night blindness and progresses as the retina gradually deteriorates. This seems to be more of a problem in the longhaired Dachshunds.

Glaucoma

Glaucoma is a leading cause of blindness in Doxie's, and it is caused by painful pressure that builds in the eye. This disease can be hereditary, so parents should be tested prior to breeding. Treatment for glaucoma can be medical or surgical, or both.

Keratoconjunctivitis Sicca(Keratitis)

Given a name that is hard to pronounce, but it really means "dry eye." Inadequate tear flow causes painful eye infections of a chronic nature and inflammation of the cornea and conjunctiva from drying. Causes vary from distemper to certain medications to removing the third eyelid tear gland. It may lead to painful corneal ulcerations in the acute stage of the disease. This is often treated with cyclosporine drops and or an ointment called cyclosporine topical therapy. Signs to look for are chronic redness of the eye, development of a film over the cornea, thick, yellow or green discharge, and decreased vision.

Hemorrhagic gastroenteritis

This is a problem of unknown origin that comes on suddenly with vomiting and diarrhea, both usually with blood. To diagnose, many other illnesses must first be eliminated through extensive blood, x-ray, urinalysis and other testing. The Dachshund will be extremely ill and without treatment will die. Once the diagnosis has been made, the dog will be given IV fluids. The IV fluids must begin immediately to prevent dehydration and then medication is added. Without the IV, the dog will die in spite of medication so get to your vet as soon as you think there might be a problem. At this time, the exact cause of this disease is unknown. There are many theories - diet, a bacterial infection or bacterial toxin, virus, reaction to an intestinal parasite, etc. - but nothing has been proven. Stress may play a role in the development of HGE. Dogs that have an episode of HGE may be prone to another occurrence.

Seborrhea

This is a hereditary skin disease which causes itching and scratching. You will notice usually dry and flaky coat, and the dog will have an odor. The Sebaceous glands will produce a waxy, oily substance in the armpits, in the ears, under the dog and around the elbow joints. Secondary ear and skin infections are common. There are many, many causes and if the vet can identify one and treat it, you're lucky. It's a tough disorder to pinpoint.

Malassezia dermatitis

This is a highly itchy skin infection, usually around the ears, muzzle, inner thighs, eyes or feet. The dog may become frantic, chewing and scratching the ears and feet. It is often associated with inflamed skin, a yellowish-grey greasy scale, dark pigmentation of the skin, self-trauma, and hair loss (alopecia) If an ear infection, there might be a waxy discharge and smelly odor. The dog will be rubbing and pawing at the ear. This seems to be more common in the summer, humidity and allergy seasons. Your vet will treat this with appropriate medications and bathing after a diagnosis.

Interdigital dermatitis

An infection that occurs between the "toes" of the Doxie which causes sacs to fill with pus that is painful to the dog. The dog licks and bites at the bothersome infections and after a few days, they break open and drain, giving relief to the Dachshund. All you will most likely notice is the dog limping around. Clean and cleanse the infected feet well, see a vet for medication to prevent returning infections.

Urolithiasis

Excessive crystals that form in the urinary tract, kidney, bladder or urethra, which block the flow of urine flow. The crystals or stones irritate the lining of the urinary tract. They cause blood in the urine and pain and in severe cases make urination impossible for the Dachshund. Symptoms are frequent urination, urinating in odd places, and blood in urine, dribbling, depression, weakness, straining, pain, vomiting and loss of appetite. Dogs can be treated by diet, medications and surgery, depending on the dog, severity and other circumstances of the individual case.

Mitral stenosis (Mitral valve insufficiency)

This seems to be a hereditary heart problem in the Dachshund. A weak mitral valve allows blood to flow backwards and to simplify this, the net result is an enlarged heart and when the heart can no longer compensate, look for a loss of desire for exercise, trouble breathing, coughing at night and liquid in the lungs. As this disease progresses, the dog may collapse. There is no cure however, the sooner this is diagnosed the quicker a vet may be able to make the dog more comfortable with medication and diet.

Diabetes

The pancreas manufactures the hormone INSULIN. If the pancreas stops making, or makes less than the normal amount of insulin, or if the tissues in the body become resistant to the insulin, the result is called "diabetes." The Doxie cannot control her blood sugar without injections of insulin on a regular basis, but given the insulin, the Dachshund can live a normal life just like a human can. If the dog does not receive the insulin injections at the same time each day of her life, the dog will go into a coma and she will die. Some causes of diabetes may be chronic pancreatitis, heredity, obesity or old age, but no one is sure. Symptoms to look for are excess drinking, urination, dehydration, weight loss, increased appetite, weight gain, and cataracts may develop suddenly. Treatment is in the form of the insulin injections daily and a strict diet low in carbohydrates and sugars. Home cooking may be suggested in many cases, which I am a great believer of in general. Frequent trips to the vet for blood monitoring will be needed but kits are sold to do this at home, and with some practice you will be able to do it.

Pancreatitis

This can be a life-threatening disease commonly affecting middle age and older dogs. The pancreas produces enzymes that help process food. The disease causes the pancreas to begin digesting its own tissue. Signs to look for are vomiting, diarrhea, loss of appetite and abdominal pain follow in most cases. Some dogs will die from lack of response to treatments. You can prevent this disease by not allowing the dog to become obese, and not giving high-fat foods to the dog.

Cutaneous asthenia

This is a hereditary, but rare disease that causes abnormally stretchy, fragile skin that tears at the slightest scratch causing scars and wounds little bleeding results and the torn areas heals with irregular scars resulting. Signs of this problem are numerous lesions of the skin, broad thin scars on the skin, gaping bleeding wounds, stretchy thin and fragile skin, and skin folds behind the elbows. The disease reveals during the first 6 months of the animal's life. A skin biopsy is used for diagnosis. Your vet will advise what can be done, if anything, depending on the individual case.

Epilepsy

A serious seizure disorder that usually appears at around 2 to 4 or 5 years of age.. If you see your Dachshund suddenly go stiff, and begin shaking it is having a seizure. This is very treatable with medication. Seizures can last a few seconds to several minutes long, remain calm, pet your Doxie, and speak softly, so that the dog doesn't panic.

Patellar luxation

Look for signs of limping, dog holding hind leg up, or your dog seems unable to straighten back leg. This is caused by an unusually shallow spot on the femur, weak ligaments and misalignment of tendons and muscles that align the knee joint and allow the knee cap (patella) to float sideways in and out of position. This can be caused by injury or be present at birth and can affect both rear legs. I have personally had one of my dogs with this problem, in both hind legs, and surgery worked wonderful.

Gastric Torsion

This is also known as twisted stomach or bloat. Symptoms include excessive drooling, nervous pacing, agitation, weakness, attempting to vomit, bulging stomach area, heavy breathing, retching and gagging, shock or total collapse. This happens when the stomach twists on itself, thus cutting off the blood supply to several organs, requiring immediate help from a vet, otherwise it will be fatal. Looks for signs that your Dachshund is pacing, salivating, acting upset, nervous or in obvious pain. It is believed that this is caused by the Doxie eating and or drinking too quickly.

Anal sac adenocarcinoma

This is a malignant tumor in the tissue of the anal sac sometimes found in the Dachshund and it's very aggressive in nature. Small tumors of this cancer are located by rectal exams by the vet. If not treated, these tumors will metastasize to lymph nodes and spread quickly to other organs. If this develops into hypocalcaemia, you'll notice an increased thirst, urination, loss of appetite, weight loss, vomiting and a slow heart rate and "scooting.". Naturally the larger the tumor, the poorer the final prognosis, therefore take your Doxie to the vet immediately upon suspecting any kind of problem. Supplements with green tea help promote a properly functioning immune system that protects against cancer and infections.

Deafness

This can be hereditary or caused by things like excessive loud noise, intolerance to anesthesia, drug toxicity, and Otitis which is a middle ear infection. In some cases, one ear can have no hearing from birth and the other ear can be losing the ability to hear over time, undetected, then suddenly one morning the hearing is totally gone. There is no reversing once that happens, and this seems to happen more so in the dapples.

Mass Cell Tumors

Mast cells are found throughout the body and help maintain the dog's normal immune response, health and body functions. The tumors are cancer and spread through the body. There is no known cause for mast cell cancer and no cure, other than surgery for early-detected, low degree tumors that haven't spread too far. The best formula is to keep the dog as healthy as possible and be aware of any signs of tumors or poor health. Whether the Dachshund survives a mast cell tumor or not depends on how advanced and fast moving the malignant tumor is.

Cleft Palate

During the growth of an unborn puppy, there may be some growth failure in the palatal area of the mouth. Cleft palate is a congenital disease of puppies where the left and right halves of the roof of the mouth fail to join together before birth. Such fusion defects are seen in a more severe form as "hare lip", where the split continues up into the nostrils. All puppies' mouths should be examined within 12 hours of birth. Mild fusion defects may not be spotted initially, but will become noticeable in those puppies that fail to suck vigorously and may have milk coming down their noses while attempting to nurse. The cause of this defect is believed to be associated with recessive genes. Although corrective surgery is possible, most breeders agree that euthanasia is indicated in a very young puppy with this defect.

Cryptorchidism

This is the failure of one or both testes to descend from the abdomen to their adult site in the scrotum. Some puppies have both testes descended at birth, but in others, the testes may not pass down into the scrotum until several weeks after birth. In the normal puppies, both testes can be found in the scrotum by 8 to 10 weeks of age. Dachshunds seem to be more susceptible to this genetic failure than other breeds. Castration is usually advised, as the testes in the abdomen are at a higher temperature and may later become diseased.

Fatty Tumors (Lipomas)

When fat cells grow without control and form lumps, they're called fatty tumors or lipomas. Dachshunds, like many dogs, are prone to develop fatty tumors. When you find unusual lumps in the skin, let your veterinarian perform some simple tests to confirm that these are not harmful growths. Holistic veterinarians may prescribe herbs that help dissolve fatty tumors, but careful consideration should be made to diet changes.

Obesity

It is important to watch your dachshund's diet as you do not want your dog to get overweight, the extra pounds only puts strain on the spine and these dogs are predisposed to slipped or ruptured disks. Regular exercise should be a part of any dachshund health program. If you notice weight gain, alter your Doxie's food, and get the weight off immediately.

Hypothyroidism

This is low thyroid hormone levels caused when the thyroid doesn't secrete enough of its hormone and is easily treated with prescription medications. Some veterinarians believe the likelihood of hypothyroidism is reduced markedly if Dachshunds are not over-vaccinated. Look for signs of weight gain, fatigue, dry skin, and hair loss.

Feeding your Dachshund Hound

Feeding a Dachshund Hound the proper well-balanced diet is important, which will give your dog a happier, longer, healthier life. Due to improper nutrition, dogs can suffer from vomiting, belching, loose stools; gassiness and stomach ache after meals. More severe problems include changes in heart rate, electrolyte imbalances, seizures, poisoning, weight gain and death. To give your Doxie a healthy life, you need to be conscientious about what you feed him. If you are "what you eat", then the same holds for your dog. All of the ads for the different dog foods on the market have left many dog owners confused, because of the varieties, prices, and claims each of them make. Doxies seem to suffer from intestinal disorders, itching, seizures, diabetes, and weight gain along with skin problems due to allergies, which in my opinion are usually causing directly by what they are eating. These problems usually start internally.

As a responsible Doxie owner, I know that you will want to provide your pet with meals that contain proteins, carbohydrates, fatty acids, vitamins, and minerals, and I just don't believe that you can get all of that in a commercial bag of dog food. Believe it or not, some of the highest priced dog foods aren't much better than the cheaper ones; and in good conscience I couldn't recommend any of them. It would be easy for me to endorse one of these companies, and sit back and collect money from them, but I can't, I love dogs too much.

I believe in a complete homemade diet, especially for a breed like the Dachshund Hound. Home-cooked food can do wonders for the dog, its teeth, and skin and hair coat, and I promise you results that you will noticeably see. It is much easier to control your dog's calorie intake when you are making the meal yourself. Cooking for your Doxie is well worth the time and effort.

Commercial dog foods can contain preservatives, additives, artificial colors and favors, residues of pesticides, toxic chemicals, filler ingredients, waste, restaurant grease, moldy grains, and low-grade meats, which can seriously have an adverse affect on your Doxie's heath. There have been several dog food recalls due to these problems, more than most people are even aware of. You will end up paying more money for these dog foods, than it will ever cost you to feed your Dachshund by cooking for it. It is important that you feed your Doxie a proper diet, and know by memory the foods that your dog should eat, and should never eat. Since Doxies are small in size, chemicals and toxins have a severe reaction on them, and to their health. I personally blame commercial dog food for being the direct cause of seizures in my own dogs. All seizures completely stopped when I fed them a homemade diet, which I believe proves my case for cooking homemade food. Although I would love to go into details here about a complete homemade food diet, the space allotted here for this book will not allow it. I wrote a book several years ago, called _"Woofing it Down",_ which is the complete quick and easy guide to making healthy dog food at home. This book will give you lists on the foods you should feed your dog, and lists of foods that you should never feed your dog. It has over 50 easy recipes, including meals, healthy treats, cakes and dog ice cream, which are easy to make. If you follow my directions, you will only need to cook for your Doxie once or twice a month, freezing their meals. I have heard from many people that purchased the book, followed the diet and told me how their dog's chronic illness improved after being fed a healthy homemade diet of fresh foods.

Please understand that you cannot make an instant change to your

Doxie puppy's diet, they are extremely sensitive to change, which can cause stress, and turn into Hypoglycemia. What I recommend you doing is start off feeding the food your puppy was eating when you purchased it. Gradually make the change from commercial dog food to homemade food by mixing them together, each week adding more homemade food, and less commercial dog food, until after a few weeks you have weaned your puppy off of that stuff, and it is only eating homemade food.

I want to be clear with you that I am not using this book as an avenue to sell my other book. Woofing it Down, has had strong sales, and has even been picked up, and translated into Portuguese to be sold in Brazil and other countries. Although I don't have the room to go into the details that you will need to feed a complete homemade diet here, I do want to at least give you enough information to get you started. Below you will find two meal recipes, and one treat recipe. I also recommend that your Doxie take a daily vitamin supplement, and add a few drops of omega fish oil.

If you are totally against cooking for your Dachshund, please make sure that you read all labels on the dog food you are feeding, and stay away from the super cheap supermarket brands, they are no bargin. Look for any signs that your Doxie is having a negative reaction, and change brands when you notice a problem.

Since Dachshund's have so many problems that are directly associated with weight gain, which ends up causing diabetes, and then the extra weight creates back problems , I highly recommend that you stick with the lower fat recipes, that use chicken or turkey, and stay away from the beef ones.

Doggie Chicken Meatloaf

Ingredients:
2 pounds of Ground Chicken (you can make this using ground turkey)
2 cups of string beans
2 cups of corn meal
1 cup of oatmeal

2 teaspoons ground eggshells (finely ground into a powder) (for added calcium)
3 eggs

Directions:
In a large mixing bowl, mix all the ingredients together blending well. Bake at 350 degrees for about 1 hour 15 minutes. You can bake this using a few loaf pans, or you can do it the way I do it. I use a large cooking sheet that has an inch-raised side (to catch the grease run off), and shape into a nice big meatloaf; this gives you more control over how wide you want to make the meatloaf. If you decide to form one big meatloaf you may need to bake for an additional 15 minutes.
Cool and cut into slices. To serve, break the meatloaf slice into small bite size chunks with a fork. I like to wrap individual slices, put into Ziploc bags and freeze, so I always have dog food on hand.

Chicken & Cellophane noodles a la doggie

Ingredients:
1 whole roasting chicken (large)
½ cup milk (lactose free)
1 package of cellophane noodles
2 hard-boiled eggs
1 teaspoon ground eggshells
½ cup oatmeal
½ box of frozen corn or mixed vegetables

Directions: Preheat oven to 350 degrees. Cut up the chicken, place in a deep pot, barely cover with water and simmer until meat is tender when you poke it with a fork. De-bone the chicken and set aside; reserve the broth. Cook the cellophane noodles in the broth according to package directions, usually 10 minutes. Mix together the chicken, noodles, eggs and vegetables in a casserole dish, pour ½ cup of milk over it and top with oatmeal. Bake for 10 minutes. Let cool and place individual servings into Ziploc Baggies and freeze.

Peanut Butter Dog Bones

Ingredients:
1-¼ cups of whole-wheat flour
½ cup quick oats oatmeal
1 egg
½ cup white flour
¾-powdered milk
¼ cup cornmeal
1/3-cup vegetable oil
3 tablespoons of unsalted natural peanut butter

Directions: Preheat oven to 350 degrees. In a large mixing bowl, mix all ingredients well. Roll out dough on a floured board and cut out shapes using cookie cutters. You can use any shape cookie cutter you want, your Doxie doesn't care if it's in the shape of a Christmas tree. Bake on cookie sheets for 16 to 18 minutes or until dry. These should be stored in an airtight container. Just remember that these have no preservatives, therefore they will go moldy or stale in just a few days. I recommend that when you make a batch, you freeze most of them, and take a few out to defrost as needed. Remember this is not a meal, this is a treat, and should only be used as such, we want to keep the weight off of the dog, not add it on.

Traveling with your Dachshund Hound

If you are planning a vacation, you need to consider whether or not you will bring your Dachshund Hound along. Traveling with your Doxie can be great, if you make all the right arrangements beforehand. Poor planning can ruin your vacation, so if you think it would be best for your dog to stay home, hire a good pet sitter, or even better get a relative that knows your dog to come stay at your home, or have your Doxie stay with them. You can also find a good kennel where you can board it. Generally Doxies are very attached to their family, and do not like being left behind, and usually refuse to eat when left in a kennel situation, therefore unless it's a real emergency, I don't recommend it.

If you are taking your Doxie with you, you'll need to bring a harness and leash that has current identification tags on it. This breed is one that is commonly stolen due to its monetary value, and most will go with anyone that offers them attention.

If you are getting to your destination by air there are a few things you should know. Canines are not cargo however; they can be considered just that by some of the airlines. Traveling in the cargo department is not a pleasant or relaxing trip for your Doxie, and I don't recommend it. Most airlines will allow you to bring a small dog, such as a mini Doxie in a pet carrier if that carrier can fit under the seat in front of you. Make sure you ask all the details before you book your flight with any airline, and find one that allows your dog onboard with you in a carrier. I have flown with a dog before, and once the plane was in the air, I pulled the carrier out from under the seat, and placed my dog on my lap. I had no complaints from any of the other passengers or even the stewardess's, as they walked down the aisles. I got a little nervous when I saw the pilot had left the cockpit and was walking towards me, until I realized that he had a smile on his face. He stopped and spoke with me about his own dog, and told me that one of the stewardess's had told him how adorable mine was, and he just needed to come back and have a look at it.

If you are planning travel by car it is usually very easy on your Doxie. The earlier your dog gets used to riding in the car, the better. Some dogs can have anxiety over riding in automobiles, because they relate it to unpleasant experiences, such as vet visits or trips to the groomers, which is why you need to make those experiences as pleasant as possible. The more positive experiences your Doxie has riding in the car, the more likely it will be to enjoy the rides. Start taking your puppy for short; frequent car rides that end at the park, or pet store where you purchase a special treat or new toy, or another fun place like a relative's home.

You should plan on making rest stops every 3 hours, so that your Dachshund can go potty, have a drink of water, and walk around on a leash for a few minutes.

Some items that you will want to bring along in the car are, harness, leash, dog carrier with a cuddly blanket inside, dog seat belt, water bowl, treats, a few toys, dog bed, bottled water that you have kept in a small travel cooler, and food that will not spoil for your dog to eat. If you are planning on stopping in restaurants to eat, and have your Doxie on a homemade food diet, you can ask them to prepare something simple, like a plain hamburger, no bun, or a grilled plain chicken breast and a vegetable that you know your dog enjoys. Please do not leave your Doxie in the car unattended while you go into eat, if possible, take the dog with you in a carrier, and stow it under the table. Naturally any medication that your dog takes should also be with you.

If you are planning on staying in a hotel, make sure that you have called in advance to know that they are pet-friendly. Some hotel and motels even offer special dog beds, dog spas, and doggie day care. Most of these hotels will charge a non-refundable pet deposit upon check in, and then a daily pet fee, which is a small price to pay to have your Dachshund Hound with you.

Spaying or Neutering

If you have no intentions of ever showing or breeding your Dachshund, you should spay or neuter it. Both operations lead to improved long-term health, prevent unwanted litters, and eliminate many behavior problems associated with the mating instinct.

Contrary to what many people think, having just one litter, does not improve the behavior of a female dog. The mating instinct may lead to undesirable behaviors and result in undue stress on the owner and the dog. Having a litter of Doxie puppies involves a lot of work, monitoring the mother's pregnancy, helping with the delivery of puppies, caring for newborn puppies, and financial expense.

During the surgical altering, a veterinarian removes the ovaries, fallopian tubes, and uterus in a female, and the testicles in the male. While both spaying and neutering are considered major surgical procedures, they are also the most common surgeries performed by vets on dogs. These operations are done painlessly while your Dachshund is comfortable under general anesthesia. After the surgery your Doxie will experience some discomfort from the normal healing process, which should be controlled with pain medication. You will need to keep your Doxie quiet and calm for a few days until the incision heals.

The benefits to your female is that she will not have to experience the heat cycle, approximately every six months, which can last as long as 21 days. During this time, your Dachshund Hound will leave bloodstains in the house, and become anxious, possibly short-tempered and will actively seek a mate. Spaying reduces the negative behaviors that lead to owner frustration, plus early spaying of a female Doxie helps protect it from serious health problems later in life such as uterine infections and breast cancer. Also you'll no longer have annoying or menacing suitors to contend with while she is having her cycle.

The male dog can generally be capable of breeding between 6-9 months of age. Male dogs are likely to begin marking their territories by spraying strong smelling urine on your furniture, curtains, and other places in your house. If given the slightest chance for escape from the home, to roam and search for a mate, they will take it. Some males seeking a female in heat can become aggressive and injure themselves and humans by engaging in fights. Therefore neutering a male Doxie reduces the breeding instinct and can have a calming effect that makes them content to stay at home with their human family. Neutering also improves the male's health by reducing the risk of prostate disease, testicular cancer, and infections.

Spaying and neutering can be performed at almost any age, but it is better done early, around six months of age. Most vets recommend that a female be spayed before her first heat cycle (around 6 months of age), and a male should be neutered around 6 months to a year old.

Please understand that these procedures will have no effect on your pet's intelligence or ability to learn, or play. Most pet owners find that they have better behaving Doxies following these operations, making them better family pets. Pets that have been spayed or neutered tend to be more gentle and affectionate, because they are less interested in other animals, and spend more time with their human family. Contrary to popular myth, having your female spayed, or your male neutered will not make it fat, because removing the ovaries or testicles does not have any effect on the dog's metabolism itself. A well balanced diet and exercise will keep your Doxie at the proper weight, during each stage of its life. Dachshund Hounds will always struggled not to be overweight, and will put on weight only if they are being overfed. This is a breed that should take regular walks daily, for the exercise benefits.

Fees for spaying and neutering vary from one area to another, largely depending on the economics of the veterinary hospital and community. This is a lifetime investment in your dog that can solve a number of potential problems for you and your Doxie. Having your pet spayed or neutered is a part of responsible dog ownership, and some breeders will insist on it when they sell you a puppy.

Before You Breed

The only reason you should breed is to improve the breed itself. Most show exhibitors breed their Dachshund Hounds for this reason, and when they do so they are looking for a litter of show dogs. You should never breed a Doxie just to have puppies for your kids to witness the miracle of life, for your female to just experience having one litter, or for the sole purpose of financial gain.

You will notice that throughout this section, I will refer to the "bitch" as female or dam. Although "bitch" is the correct technical term for a female dog, I personality find it offensive and degrading, and believe that word should be used in reference only when one is speaking about their mother-in-law.

Breeding is not an easy thing to do, and you will not have money rolling in from just allowing your dogs to do what comes naturally. There is much to learn about breeding Doxies and I will tell you the good and the bad. I have bred for many years, so I speak from genuine experience and have all the knowledge you seek. I admit that it was one of the most rewarding things I have ever done in my life, and I feel like each and every puppy was like a child of mine. After reading this chapter if you still decide that breeding is for you, I promise that you will gain much joy, happiness, satisfaction and wonderful memories.

Breeding Doxies is difficult, and I will provide you will all the information that you will need, but be prepared for hard work. There are many things that you will need to know before you mate, also things that can happen because of breeding, and items that you must have during the birthing and afterwards, so that you will be completely prepared. Breeding your Doxie is not risk free, every time you have a litter; you risk something happening to you pet.

Breeding Dachshund Hounds is not a moneymaking venture; in fact you will be lucky if you break even, that is the reality. The average litter size for a Doxie can be between 1 –6 puppies. You might be thinking about all the money you will get for selling these precious puppies, but you also need to take into account the expenses that you should expect to occur. Raising a litter of Dachshund Hound puppies will cost money, and if you have unexpected problems, it's going to cost you even more. An example of your expenses would be stud fee (if you don't own the male), this is usually the cost of one of the puppies to be sold or pick of the litter. Whelping box, a hard plastic kiddie swimming pool (which I highly recommend) heating pad or heat lamp, thermometer, scissors, towels, baby scale, tweezers, baby suction bulb, hemostats, puppy milk replacement formula, puppy baby bottles, and nail clippers. Other things to take into consideration would be vet trips to have the puppies de-wormed, dewclaws removed, and vaccinations. The mother should also be vet checked during the pregnancy and then again after giving birth. You can also expect the mother to eat up to three times what she normally eats while she is nursing the puppies.

You will have other costs that you probably haven't even thought about. Your female should have an ultrasound the week before giving birth, so that you know how many puppies you can expect her to have. This way if you know she is having 3 puppies, and only delivers 2, you will need to take her to the vet within an hour, if the last puppy doesn't arrive. You could also have an emergency vet trip, if your female is unable to give birth, and requires a c-section or an emergency trip to save a puppy that is in danger of dying. Your female could end up with mastitis, an infection of her breast during the nursing time, and require a vet visit for antibiotics. The costs of advertising in the newspaper to sell the puppies aren't cheap either. You are probably wondering, if people aren't making money doing this, why do they breed, the only answer is because it's a labor of love. I'm not saying that it isn't possible to get lucky once in a while, and come out with a reasonable profit; I'm saying that if done properly, it's doubtful. If you have read the above, and still want to breed, please continue on.

Before you breed, ask yourself if your female is true show quality, has earned her championship, is free from any hereditary diseases, and mature enough to breed. If the answer is yes to all of the questions, continue on.

Do you have homes set already for the puppies before the mating or will you be able to sell them without a problem? If you aren't able to find homes for these puppies, are you able and willing to keep all of them? Are you prepared to offer the puppies buyers a lifetime guarantee for the health of the puppies (or at least one year), and are you prepared to take them back if necessary, and find another home? Will you demand that any non-show quality puppy be sold with a spay/neuter agreement? Are you prepared to fully screen each and every person that desires to purchase a puppy from you? Will you be able to part with the puppies that you have raised for the last 12 weeks and become emotionally attached to? Do you have the money you need in case of an emergency c-section, or any other complications even if this means you lose all your puppies and get no income from selling them? Are you fully prepared to spend most of the first couple of weeks of the puppy's lives without much sleep?

There are no guarantees, breeding your Dachshund, is putting her at risk. It doesn't matter how many times you have done this, unexpected things can happen. Even the death of one pup, can be heartbreaking. You must always hope for the best, but be prepared for the worse.

Pregnancy is a huge health issue for many Dachshunds because of the additional pressure it puts on the back as well as problems with whelping because they have a longer birth canal. Always talk to your vet before deciding if this is the right thing for you and your dog. Many female Dachshunds have difficulty in conceiving and may require artificial insemination in order to become pregnant. This is not a costly procedure but it is an added expense that owners and potential breeders need to consider.

It's a good idea to have someone that has done this before in your corner. You can get advice from the breeder you purchased your Doxie from, a dog club, a breeder you have met at a dog show, or the owner of the stud you are planning to use. If its possible assist in the birthing of someone else's Dachshund Hound litter before you decide to start breed yourself, I highly recommend it. That will give you a better idea of what to expect, because if you have never assisted in the whelping of a litter before, you are going to find out that it is significantly harder and more stressful than you originally thought.

Take your time to learn and study the pedigrees of the Doxies you have seen at the shows, this will help you chose the stud to breed your female with.

As a final note if you decide to breed your Dachshund Hound without the proper care, then the responsibility for a bad outcome will rest on your own shoulders.

Line Breeding & Inbreeding & Outcrossing Breeding

There are several different methods to picking your stud, and depending on whom you talk to you, you'll get different answers about what is best. I believe what really matters are the quality of the two dogs in question, not the formula by which they are bred. The reason I say that is because commonly two puppies from the exact same litter can be completely different, one being top show quality, and the other poor pet quality you can't control nature.

Line Breeding means breeding two dogs that are relatives of each other together. Many different animal species line breed naturally. The reason many breeders will decide to line breed, is because they are planning for the set characteristics in the progeny. This is not an exact science, therefore sometimes the characteristics you wanted the puppies to inherit just don't happen, and while other recessive hidden ones do. Usually by line breeding you know what to expect. If your dog has health problems within the line, you would be further setting those health problems by line breeding, and therefore would want to avoid it. Line breeding is simply weak inbreeding, so it does still carry all the problems of both out crossing and inbreeding. I believe that the degree of the relationship does not necessarily indicate the amount of genetic material shared. Again, puppy mates from the same litters can be completely different from each other. You must pick a mate wisely based on depth of knowledge of what those pedigree lines of each mean, and what characteristics both dogs likely share, the good and the bad.

Out crossing is when you take two unrelated Dachshund Hound lines, and breed them together. This is risky business, because you have no idea what you are going to get with this type of breeding. You are basically breeding random pedigree Doxies to each other, and will have no idea what the babies are going to look like. You may or may not get the best characteristics of the mother or the father by doing this kind of breeding, and will most likely end up with pet quality puppies. However, this is the best way to deal with some genetic problems, when you have a problem in your own line, you can do this to breed out of that problem. You do have to understand that you will never breed out of a problem completely, because it is genetic, it will still be there in the line, perhaps just hidden. Outcross should be done when you need to bring things into your line, but know that some unseen other things will accompany the traits that you desire. The best outcrosses are usually Doxies from two separate families with similar traits. I'm sure that many out crossings wouldn't even be that if extended pedigrees were viewed, many breeds with successful bloodlines go back to each other, and will have same relatives.

Inbreeding will bring some very bad things out in your line. Things that you already know are there. The closer the breeding, the better the two dogs must be to make it work. Breeding dogs closely related is inbreeding, the point is to double up on desired line characteristics by doubling up on the genes. However, everything recessive in the family will creep up eventually by doing this if line breeding is done over generations.

Breeding Up means basically using a well-known dog to a poor quality female in hopes that the offspring will better from it. This is a bad idea, but it often happens. The outcome is nearly always the same; the owners of the new puppies will find that they aren't much better than the poor quality mother. The worst part of this is, the high quality show dog stud now has a reputation for creating poor quality pups.

Breeding Pedigrees means breeding based on their paper pedigree or breeding based solely on a famous dog's popularity or show records. One cannot take the parents show records into the ring to convince the judge of the merits of their offspring, when your dog is in the ring, it will stand on its own merit, you cannot make your stud selection based on fame, reputation or an ad for the deciding factor in a breeding partner. Breeding must be done seeing the sire and the dam together, by their respective families when it comes to flaws, and then standing alone when it comes to what virtues they can potentially offer the other. In being honest, there is just no perfect recipe for breeding dogs, and no substitute for a well-trained experienced eye, and certainly no shame in asking for the help of someone that really knows what they are doing.

Casual breeding produces more than ¾ of all the registered pedigree dogs in the United States. It seems that everyone is breeding their own registered pet, without the serious study necessary to breed dogs well enough to avoid bad temperaments and health problems. They often do not know or understand that major genetic problems will just continue to be passed along, as they are often indiscriminately inbred. In order to be a breeder, you must get the education, be dedicated, and force yourself to be scrupulous in your selections. Breeders need to know the dogs they are using intimately. Great and consistent bloodlines have been built on good, consistent dogs bred by knowledgeable breeders. Knowledge is the key, knowing in depth what you are breeding. This means understanding the basics of inheritance, and knowing how to apply them for the best results in your breeding practices. I understand that you must learn as you go, but please read before you breed and talk to others at the shows, learn from them before you start creating lives. Any stud owner that you approach should have the knowledge to help you decide if you are making a good match.

WARNING about breeding dapples to dapples, this will result in Double Dapple Defects. There are lethal genes commonly associated with double dapple. Not all double dapples have these problems and it is believed by some to be more of a problem in some lines than in others. The problems associated with lethal genes in double dapples there are varying degrees of vision and hearing loss, including reduced or absent eyes. So if you decide that you want a double dapple puppy, be prepared for possible problems that may not be diagnosed at a young age, and if you want to breed a double dapple interestingly if a blind or deaf double dapple is bred to a normal dog, the lethal traits are not passed on to the offspring, however most of the puppies of the double dapple will be dapple. Remember that single dapple dachshunds do not have lethal problems and if a single dapple is bred to a solid (any non-dapple) there are no problems associated with single dapple dachshunds.

The Mating

Most female Dachshund Hounds will go into heat about every 6 to 7 months, beginning sometime before their first birthday. You should expect her to be in heat for approximately three weeks. You should never breed on the first heat wait until the second cycle which many consider to be the time when she has the greatest fertility.

Your female should be ready to stand and hold for the male to mount and breed her about ten to twelve days into the heat cycle. You should start counting days at the first sign of any blood discharge from the vulva. You will want to keep an eye on her attitude and temperament, and know that you could have missed a few days of a light flow. Keep in mind that every Doxie will be a little different as far as when she will accept the male. So when you bring her to the male for breeding, don't wait until the tenth day, bring her a few days ahead of time, because she may be ready. Your Doxie will let you know if you have the correct timing by her willingness or unwillingness to stand for the stud. If she's ready, she will pull her tail to one side; stand in front of the male, and sometimes even back into him. You will also note that when it is time to breed, her discharge will turn from a dark, bloody color to a lighter tan color. Always bring the pair together sooner than you believe is the peak of her cycle, it is better to be a few days too early than a day too late, because she will not be in heat again for another 6 months. If they don't mate on the first try, at least the two have met each other, and will do so in another day or two. I always recommend taking your female to the stud, as he will be more likely to perform in his own environment.

During the process the dogs will lock up or tie. This can last anywhere from two minutes to up to 45 minutes depending on the dog. This is the time that the male's sperm is actually being released. Make sure that you are around; some Doxie females can panic during this time, and attempt to run, dragging the male along, which can cause serious injury to him. Most stud owners will insist on being there during the breeding, because they know that this kind of an injury can happen and end their own stud dogs breeding career. You can expect that the stud's owner will do most of the supervising during the breeding, let them do it, they have the experience, and this is part of what you are paying them to do. You will most likely be asked to calm and comfort your dog during the tie up, just pet her, and talk to her until the two break free. In this bred the pair will usually end up butt to butt during this process, still hooked together, just relax, this is normal and neither of them is being hurt. You will want to mate your female to the male the following day. Usually two matings are enough to allow pregnancy, certainly never more than three. If all goes well, the sperm will fertilize the eggs and the fertile eggs will migrate down the two uterine horns in search for a favorable area to attach to the lining of the uterine wall. Attachment occurs a few days after the breeding.

You don't want to over breed your dog, or you will end up with a large litter that she will not be able to carry, risking her uterus rupturing and losing your dog and all the pups. Over breeding is a common mistake that first timers make, because they are so anxious to make sure their dog gets pregnant. Doxies are capable of getting pregnant on each and every mating session. You can have a litter of puppies from which several of them have been conceived on different days, thus this causes the puppies from the last mating to be born pre-mature. While it is true that we often learn from our mistakes, I hope that by reading this book, I can spare you from making the same ones that I did. You do not want your dog carrying a double litter, and trust me; I know from experience that she will not be able to care for all the puppies, that is if they even survive being born. Breeding can be exciting and extremely rewarding, when it's done properly. To have the opportunity to witness the changes in newborn puppies each day, when they first open their eyes, the first wobbly steps they take, the first bark, and their first solid meal, and finally the happiness they bring to the new family they go home with are pure joy.

The Pregnancy

You won't know for a few weeks if your female has become pregnant. If it has been a successful breeding, you will notice a slight increase in her appetite. You'll start to see a slight increase in nipple size, and then naturally the next step, she will start to show. During this exciting time, you will want to increase her food intake, but you do not want to make her obese, which would lead to whelping complications, and back problems. Extra calcium should be added into her diet plan; she will need it when it comes time to nurse her puppies. If you don't already have her on a daily vitamin, this would be a great time to start her on one.

The gestation time for a Doxie is anywhere between 58-63 days, make sure you mark your calendar from the date of the first mating, and be prepared to be with her during that entire time, this means, don't leave the house!! Understand that if you bred her multiple times, you don't know for sure when her due date is. In my own experience, Doxies seem to go around the 60 days mark, but you must be prepared for it to happen earlier.

One of my fondest memories of breeding, was placing my pregnant dog on her back, and gently rubbing her mommy belly. You will see all the little bumps, and bubble movements from the puppies, its' very exciting to witness and feel such activity.

I recommend that one week before the due date, you take her to the vet for a quick sonogram or x-ray (don't worry, one single x-ray taken of full term puppies is safe). I like to know how many puppies she has inside, so that I know they have all come out, and there is no doubt when she has finished giving birth.

During this time she will appreciate more attention than usual, and towards the end, she will keep checking to make sure that you are around. I found mine liked to follow me from room to room in the house, as if she just didn't want me out of her sight.

The last two weeks of pregnancy you should limit some of her activities, like climbing stairs and, naturally with this breed you want to always discourage leaping up and down on furniture, but this will be especially true during the pregnancy. Remember that this is giving added weight on the abdomen area, putting more stress and strain on the back, so handle her with extra loving care. Avoid her being in extreme heat or extreme cold.

Whelping

Many breeders will monitor their female's temperature during the last half of the pregnancy. Some female's temperatures will drop from the normal range of 101 to 102-5 degrees to a degree or even more below normal a few hours before going into labor; however this is not always the case. From my experiences breeding, constantly taking their temperature is not only inconvenient, it's annoying and uncomfortable to your dog, and I have had no success seeing any temperature drop that was worth noting. You will see so many other signs that she is going into labor; you don't really need to be worrying about this, the hassle just isn't worth it for me.

At least two weeks before the due date, set up the whelping box, and have your dog start to get used to it. Actual wooden whelping boxes are great for larger breed dogs, however we are talking about Doxies; therefore I myself never used one. I preferred to take a regular cardboard box, and cut out the front of it, lining it with several comfortable towels. My dog would begin to use this box, as a bed during the last two weeks. After the delivery, I transferred my puppies into a plastic child swimming pool, that contained a heating pad covered with towels, which allowed the mother to jump over the side to get in, in order to care for her newborn puppies, yet, she could easily hop out of the pool to go outside to potty and take the much needed breaks from them. The puppies were safe and secure in the swimming pool, and it was easy and sanitary to clean up after them. You can place either a pillow on the outside of the pool or even a makeshift ramp to help your Doxie get in and out of the pool, if she seems to have problems hopping in and out of it.

A word of caution if you have a long hair Doxie in full show coat giving birth can be very dangerous. Puppies can easily hang themselves from a few strands of hair. During the time of delivery, it's almost impossible to work around the hair, and it will also get quite messy and soiled. You MUST wrap your Doxie's hair up BEFORE labor begins. Either put it up in ponytails, or cut it, but get it out of the way before labor begins. The hair will need to stay up for the next few weeks, as the puppies nurse.

Usually the first sign of labor will be her lack of interest in eating, approximately twenty-four hours before birth. You will also notice that she will lick at her vulva, and will most likely be experiencing abdominal cramping. She may scoot across the carpeting, not quite sure of what she is feeling, especially if it's a first time mommy. You will notice changes in her normal behavior, laying down one minute, and then the next running around, not sure what she really wants, extremely restless. Some females will insist that they see you in their vision at all times, afraid that they will be alone, while others may start to seek out a hiding place. I had one that decided she wanted to give birth behind my waterbed, which would have been a disaster, as I had no way of reaching her or her puppies. I was able to coax her out, using a tempting food tidbit, and then immediately blocked off her hiding burrow so she couldn't get behind the bed again. Thankfully this happened the day before she went into labor, as she started to seek out a good private place to hide. The last few days, you will want to keep a close eye on her.

When the abdominal contractions become strong, your Doxie should be in the whelping box. You will be able to visually see her belly contracting, and feel them when placing your hand on her belly. You can expect her to hunch in the corner of the box, almost appearing that she is having a bowel movement. On rare occasions, you will get a dog that prefers to give birth while lying on her side. Next you will notice a shiny, gray or purplish bubble appear from the vulva, it almost looks like a balloon in appearance. As soon as you witness any signs of this bubble, make note of the exact time. The female will usually push out the bubble with the next few contractions. You need to be ready at this point, make sure that the sac falls onto the towels in the box, and do not allow her to run around during this process, keep her in the box. The first puppy is usually the most difficult for her to pass, usually being the largest puppy, and she may strain hard, moan or even yelp. Most will usually pant heavily as if overheated this is normal behavior. She may bite down on the towel during this, or even tear it, which helps her relieve pain; you will want to dispose of the towels in the box after the birthing process anyways. She may dig and crawl at the towels ripping them, allow her to do this. If your Doxie doesn't pass the first puppy within one hour of seeing the water sac showing, then she is having a problem, and you need to call your veterinarian immediately, make sure you time this process.

When the pup is born, you need to quickly break and remove the sac, rub the puppy down with a dry washcloth, and get it breathing. You should NOT remove the puppy from the whelping box, it will upset the mother, instead, lean into the box, holding the puppy in front of the mother, so she can see that you are helping her, not stealing her newborn. Because Doxie puppies are so tiny, usually between 5 to 6 ounces at birth, you don't need to use a large towel; you can carefully handle them better, with a washcloth. Most dogs will bite and break the sac, and clean their own puppy, but in the case of Doxies they usually don't. This is a breed that wants and needs your help during the birthing process. Talk to your dog, pet her head, calm her, and reassure her that you are there with her, and everything is all right. Stay calm; as she will feed off of your emotions, if you are freaking out, she will believe something is wrong. Remember that you only have 5 minutes to get the puppy to begin breathing on its own, otherwise brain damage will occur.

The puppy will be attached to a mass of blackish-green tissue by the umbilical cord, which is the after birth. Some believe that it is a good idea to allow the mother to eat at least one of the afterbirths as disgusting as it sounds, but I prefer to get a hold of it, and discard it quickly before she attempts it. Usually if the mother eats it, she'll end up having severe diarrhea and an upset stomach, for several days afterwards so try to avoid it. Nature tells her to eat it, to get rid of any odors or evidence in the wild that another animal could smell, telling them that she has newborns and is in a vulnerable position. You will want to use dental floss to tie off the cord about 1 inch from the puppy, and then using a clean pairs of scissors, should cut the umbilical cord. Then immediately give the puppy back to the mother, and allow her to continue licking and cleaning the new pup. You should not remove the puppy from the mother; you must do this while leaning into the whelping box. Then place the puppy on one of the mother's nipples so it can begin to nurse. While she is caring for her puppy, the process will start all over again, and she will present another pup. Please make sure that she doesn't lie down, stand on, or stomp the puppy she has, while giving birth to the next one, especially if she insists on digging into the towels. When you can grab time in between the birthing of the puppies, place each pup on one of her nipples, as you can expect them to keep falling off of them, to allow them to continue nursing. Newborns will often need assistance locating a nipple, place their mouth directly over one, and hold them on it for a minute or two until they grab on.

Every single litter my dogs have had, happened either late evening, or in the middle of the night, so you must be prepared to watch your dog. Of course, yours could decide to give birth early in the morning. If you suspect that she is beginning labor, don't even think about going to sleep, if you need to take turns with someone else to watch her, do it, otherwise the minute to close your eyes, it will be a sure guarantee she will begin labor. The entire process can take between two hours or 5 hours, depending on how many puppies she is expecting. She may have all her puppies in the first hour; having each 10 minutes apart or she may have as long as one hour between each one, all dogs are different.

If your dog is really straining, with strong contractions every few minutes and no pup is presented, get the veterinarian on the phone; she will most likely require a c-section. In general, this breed does have problems giving birth, therefore be prepared for a c-section.

You should offer her water during this process, but hold off on food. She may vomit during the delivery, quickly clean it up, and make nothing of it. Expect that your dog will have to go potty almost immediately when she has finished giving birth to the last puppy, if she has an accident in the house, don't scold her for it. She will not want to leave her puppies to go outside, but try and get her to do it, assuring her that the puppies will be fine.

Once the mess is over, and all the puppies are contently nursing, set up the swimming pool that I spoke about. Place a heating pad (on low) under a nice fluffy clean towel, and transfer each puppy over to it. Show the mom how she can hop in and out of the swimming pool to care for her puppies. She may not want you to handle them a lot, and will get very upset if you attempt to take them away from her, resist over handling them right now. Assure her that you are helping her, and not stealing her puppies, she will be very defensive and protective of her babies. The real trick is to help her, but not interfere; it's a delicate balance you will understand after your first litter.

You will naturally be excited and want to show off your babies to family and friends. Puppies can easily become sick at this time, so you need to reframe from allowing others to touch them for the first few weeks; instead let them have a peek from a distance of a few feet away.

Call your vet and make an appointment to bring your Doxie in for a checkup and her puppies in the following day or the day after. This is the time to have the vet remove the puppy's dewclaws; it must be done within the first three days of life. When sitting in the vet's office, people will be naturally curious and delight in seeing newborn puppies, firmly tell them that you would prefer they keep their distance from them, as they are extremely susceptible to disease at this time, and they should respect that. If they think you are being rude, too bad, they will get over it, and you'll most likely never see them again. I had one man who didn't control his large German shepherd on his leash, and allowed it to stick its head over the top of the cardboard box I had carefully lined with fresh towels containing my dog with her puppies. My sweet dog, snapped, and bit the Shepherd hard in his snout. As far as I'm concerned, the owner of that dog got what he deserved, and I admit I was quite proud of my girl for protecting her babies, although the poor Shepherd did let out quite a yelp, but immediately backed off. Before you leave the vets office that day, you should make appointments for de-worming the puppies, and the puppy's first shots.

Caring for Newborns

I firmly believe that all the puppies should be picked up, cuddled, held, petted, and touched each day by the breeder. This gives the puppies important socialization skills, and it begins to understand that human touch is a good thing. The first three weeks is the hardest time, and probably the most exhausting and stressful time for you. If you are going to lose a puppy, it's usually during the first three critical weeks. You must make sure that the puppies are nursing every hour or so the first few nights and days, and that means no sleep for you. You'll need to constantly check to make sure that the mother isn't smothering her own puppies by laying down on them, or still digging thru the towels to make them comfortable for her to lay down.

The smaller pups need help locating a nipple the first few days, and must be placed on one, sometimes; you will need to hold a weak puppy on there. I like to make a rule to do this at least every two hours, more often if I see that the smaller puppy is weak, and has a thin neck, a clear sign of dehydration. They should start gaining weight, a few grams each day, please use a proper puppy scale and weigh each one daily, making sure you keep track of their weight. You must weigh your puppies, record it, and watch for any puppy that's weight is going down. A puppy should double their birth weight around 10 days old. You will want to check puppies for any signs of dehydration, to do that, lightly pinch together the skin at the back of the neck. If it stays in a crease, the puppy is dehydrating, but if when you let it go, the skin instantly springs back, the puppy is thriving. Immediately place any puppy that is in danger of dehydration onto one of the mother's nipples. The ones on the bottom have the most milk. If your puppy is not willing to nurse, or seems to be having problems, you must start bottle-feeding. I like to put a few drops of Karo corn syrup into the puppy formula, at this point your puppy really needs it, and I have found that it works wonders with fading puppies.

Puppies are born blind with their eyelids sealed shut. Never attempt to pull or open their eyes. By the time they are 2 weeks old, the eyelids will open, and the puppy will begin to develop vision.

Make sure that you trim puppy nails, so that they don't scratch and irritate the mother's skin and nipples. Your Doxie should be eating more calcium in her diet, and naturally should have fresh water available all the time, do not neglect her needs, as nursing her puppies is draining her.

I like to set up towels on one side of the swimming pool, and puppy training pads on the other. As puppies take their first few wobbling steps and explore, they are also starting to learn what area they should eliminate in. You can expect the puppies to play with their littermates, and sometimes be quite vocal. Your puppy will learn to bark around 3 to 4 weeks old, and the sound of their first squeaks and barks are adorable. Around 3 weeks old, you can give them a very shallow water dish, and allow them to begin lapping some water if they desire.

Weaning the Puppies

You can begin feeding tiny, liquidly soft food to your puppies around 6 weeks old. I like to cook for my dogs, usually starting them off with something simple like, boiled chicken and rice, water and some puppy milk formula , after cooking I place it in a blender, to create what I call puppy gruel, a paste like consistency. If you have decided that you don't want to go the homemade dog food way, than buy high quality puppy chow, and wet with water until it's soft. One of the best ways to start feeding puppies is to give them the food in a shallow pan, like a small cookie sheet. Gently place the pups around the edge of the food, and push their face into it, they will smell it and begin to lick. I must warn you that the first few meals are quite messy, as they will usually end up walking thru the food, perhaps even roll around in it, but get the camera ready; it's also very cute. At this time, the puppies should be hopping and bouncing around the swimming pool, playing with each other. They have fully developed their sight and hearing. They should still be nursing from their mom, but will slowly become more interested in eating the new tasty food you are offering them. In a few days, when they are doing well with food, you can have mom stop nursing them.

When it's time to say Goodbye

This is tough chapter to write because preparing for your dog's death is a heart wrenching situation, and something that no one ever even wants to think about but it is necessary. There is never an easy way to say your final goodbyes, and the only thing that has ever provided me some peace or comfort, is to know in my heart that one day I will be reunited with all of my dogs, on the other side at the Rainbow Bridge.

Sadly dogs don't live as long as we would like them to, and the day will come when you and your Doxie must part ways. We are never quite prepared for the death of a pet. Whether death is swift and unexpected or whether it comes at the end of a slow decline, we are never fully aware of what a dog has brought to our lives until they are gone. During the last few days of your dog's life you will want to make your pet as comfortable as possible while making the final arrangements for its burial, which will also ease some of the pain of losing your Dachshund.

You must make sure you are being realistic about your Doxies diagnoses. If your veterinarian has given you a time frame in which you can expect a loss, than use it to your advantage by making the most of your time with your dog. You can also ease your Doxies suffering by helping him be as comfortable as possible. Lavish your dog with extra hugs, kisses, attention, special treats, a favorite meal and naturally lots of love. While you are petting your Dachshund, talk to it, tell him how much he will be missed, because believe me they really do understand. Speak softly; don't place your own fears on to your Doxie. The dog already knows that something is wrong, you don't want to frighten him, let your pet know that he should not be afraid, and that it is ok for him to go. You will want to keep a positive attitude while you are around your dog. Doxies are highly sensitive animals and know when their owners are upset. Be sure and take many pictures in these last days, because you will cherish them for years to come.

Consult with your veterinarian, and don't be afraid to ask questions about treatment or care options available. It is sometimes difficult to strike a balance between your Doxie's health and its general happiness. Sometimes, treatments for diseases or injuries can substantially lower your dog's quality of life.

It is best to decide now on the arrangements for your pet's burial, because if you know your option beforehand, you'll have one less thing on your mind when your beloved dog passes on. You can choose to bury your Doxie at home in the yard, in a pet cemetery or have the body cremated keeping the ashes in an urn somewhere in your home. Only you can decide what is best for you. I have buried two in my backyard, with a beautiful stepping stone marker that has their names on it, and then planted a flowering bush over the gravesites. I also have had several of my Doxies cremated, and their ashes were placed in sealed pink marble urns, either way, I hurt deeply and cried a river of tears for each and every one of them.

Euthanasia is by far the most difficult decision that any dog owner can face, but sometimes it really is the only humane option. If your Doxie is suffering and your veterinarian recommends that you should put him to sleep, please listen. These are the dreaded words that no dog owner ever wants to hear during a vet visit but understand that doctors of veterinary medicine do not exercise this option lightly. Their medical training and professional lives are dedicated to diagnosis and treatment of disease. Veterinarians are keenly aware of the balance between extending an animal's life and its suffering. Euthanasia is the ultimate tool to mercifully end a dog's suffering. Euthanasia is the induction of painless death. In veterinary practice, it is accomplished by intravenous injection of a concentrated dose of anesthetic. The animal may feel slight discomfort when the needle tip passes through the skin, but this is no greater than any other injection. The euthanasia solution takes only seconds to induce a total loss of consciousness. This is soon followed by respiratory depression and cardiac arrest.

Everyone secretly hopes for a pet's peaceful passing, hoping to find it lying in its favorite spot in the morning. The impact of a pet's death is significantly increased when, as responsible and loving caretakers, we decide to have the pet euthanized. It is natural to look for signs of health and see them even when they aren't really there. Often dog owner's delay performing euthanasia on their dogs because they cannot bear the thought of parting with them, we may postpone the decision, bargaining with ourselves that if we wait another day, the decision will not be necessary. While this act is highly understandable, it is also extremely unfair to their dog, and quite selfish. Guilt has a way of sitting heavily on the one who must decide. The fundamental guideline is to do what is best for your dog, even if you must suffer.

There is nothing that anyone can say that will make this idea any easier, except to know that your Doxie is no longer suffering or in pain, and this is your last act of kindness and compassion towards your pet. Doing what is best for your Dachshund, your family, and the situation is a private matter. Some individuals find the process of putting their beloved pet to sleep about as peaceful as death can possibly be, and in reality, it is the most peaceful option for most animals that are suffering or have been battling a long-term illness or disability. The number one statement of concern that most pet lovers who are considering having their honored pet put to sleep is that they need to feel sure that it is the right time. Nobody wants to watch his or her dog suffer needlessly. At the same time, nobody wants to rob his or her pet of possible active and tolerable months or even years, nor are we ever truly ready to let go. I myself have made the appointment three times before I was finally able to take my dog in. This can be part of the process for some people. While this is a very difficult time for all pet owners, the absolute greatest piece of advice I have ever heard regarding the timing of putting a dog down was relatively simple; look into his eyes and trust your heart. While it certainly doesn't seem very scientific or medically sound, people who have a significant bond with their Doxie are able to understand when the "light" in his eyes has deteriorated too far. If you need the scientific part, than ask yourself the following questions, and make sure that you answer them honestly.

1. Is your Doxie's health condition prolonged, recurring or getting worse with time?
2. Is your Doxie's condition no longer responding to medical treatment or therapy?
3. Is your Doxie in constant pain or suffering physically or mentally?
4. Is it impossible to lessen your Doxie's pain or suffering?
5. If your Doxie recovers, is he likely to be chronically ill?
6. Can I provide the necessary care?
7. Can I afford the cost of medical treatment now – or over a long period of time?
8. Is your Doxie still eating well or has he lost considerable weight?
9. Is your Doxie still playful and happy?
10. Is your Doxie still affectionate towards you and others?
11. Is your Doxie interested in activity's surrounding it?
12. Does your Doxie seem tired and withdrawn most of the time?

The decision to perform euthanasia on your dog should not be yours alone. Talk to your vet and of course other family members in the household. Your Doxie is part of your family therefore the final choice should be a family decision.

If you are lucky, in some cases, your Doxie will tell you it's time. He will start to separate himself from you. If he has spent nearly every night sleeping beside, or in, your bed and he seeks out places that resemble a cave, he may be preparing himself for death. Pack animals in particular have been known to separate themselves from the pack in order to prevent the strong from becoming injured while protecting the weak, therefore pay special attention to your Doxie if it seems to be searching for a hiding spot. Whatever decision make, you know that you have acted in the best interest of your dog and that he has had a happy life with you.

The decision to be with your Doxie during the euthanasia is a personal one. While it is a simple and quite, even peaceful procedure, there is no shame in keeping his memory as he was in life. Some people feel as though they are betraying their pet by not following through to the end, only you can decide, it's a decision you must live with, without regret, forever. If you opt not to go in with your Doxie, the veterinary staff will be able to offer your dog absolutely everything he or she will need. There is no shame and there is no guilt necessary. I myself made the decision to be with my dogs during this time. I have had to make the sad decision to put down 4 of my mine during the course of my lifetime so far, something I have never regretted, as it was the right thing to do with each one of them at the time. I was able to pet their heads, kiss their snouts, and whisper that I loved them in their ear as they relaxed and went to sleep. I saw them peaceful, at rest, and no longer suffering, and because I was able to be there with them at the end, it made me feel better, and I was able to see how the process worked, and knew that they had a peaceful, quiet, relaxed death. I was given comfort and sympathies from my vet and the office staff, who understood my pain and loss. The dignity and grace shown by our dying pets may well be their last gift to us.

You will grieve for your Doxie; this is a process that will take time to get thru. For many of us who love our dogs like children, their death can affect some of us more than the death of a close relative or friend. The death of a pet leaves few people totally untouched, but there are exceptions to every rule. When a pet dies, we expect that others will acknowledge our deep pain, loss and hurt. The bond between you and your Doxie is as valuable as any of your human relationships; but other people may not always appreciate the importance of its loss. Be prepared to encounter those that will say, "Oh it was just a dog, get over it". The process of grieving for a dog is no different than mourning the death of a human being. The difference lies in the value that is placed on your pet by you alone, and others that have suffered from the same. Seek validation for your pain from people who will understand you and ones that are willing to help you during the bereavement process, and ignore the ignorance of those that will not. Remember that you do not need anyone else's approval to mourn the loss of your Doxie, nor do you have to justify your feelings to anyone. The joy found in the companionship of an animal is a blessing not given to everyone. Your life was and will continue to be brighter because of the special time you shared with your Dachshund. This is the best testament to the value of your pet's existence.

Dachshund Facts, Oddities and Interesting Tidbits

D achshund Hounds have been owned by such famous people as, John Wayne, Marlon Brando, Clark Gable, Errol Flynn, Carol Lombard, Madonna, Joan Crawford, Elizabeth Taylor, Gary Berghoff, Cindy Crawford, Gypsy Rose Lee, Gloria Swanson, Rembrandt, Michelangelo, Da Vinci, Picasso, Andy Warhol, William Shakespeare, Tom Clancy, Danielle Steele, J.D. Salinger, General George Patton, Napoleon Bonaparte, Donald Rumsfeld Secretary of Defense, and the current Queen of England, just to name a few.

It is well known that throughout the 14th, 15th, and 16th Centuries, the Catholic Popes in Rome kept hundreds of dachshunds in kennels, and bred them for use as "altar-dogs" in Catholic ceremonies.

MGM's animated children's cartoon movie "All Dogs Go to Heaven" had a Dachshund named Itchy.

Brutus, a red smooth-hair dachshund, and the only dog of any breed certified as a skydiver, fell to earth at 128 miles per hour with his loving companion who pulled the cord and opened their parachute in plenty of time to make a safe landing

The mascot of the WORLD CHAMPION American Women's World Cup Soccer Team is a Dachshund.

A Dachshund was featured in the TV Show Hogan's Heroes, starring with Bob Crane as the pet dog of Colonel Klink.

Just for Fun

So much of this book has dealt with serious subjects, and while owning a dog of any breed has its share of responsibilities, pet ownership also brings much happiness and joy. You have purchased your Dachshund Hound for enjoyment, and companionship, that's what dogs are all about, so relax, love and have fun with your new puppy.

Dachshund Hound
Patricia O'Grady

Across

2 A doxie can be smooth, wire hair or ?
4 Another name for hot dog
6 Best place to purchase a purebred puppy
7 Title earned in a dog show
9 Barks to let you know someone is at the door
11 What a Doxie can injure from jumping off a couch
12 Which of the seven groups is the Dachshund in?

Down

1 What do you call a doctor that cares for animals?
2 Favorite place for a Dachshund to sit?
3 Country of Origin of a Dachshund Hound
5 What a puppy does when losing it's teeth
8 To have a female surgically altered
10 Food nickname for a Dachshund Hound

DACHSHUND HOUND
Patricia O'Grady

E	G	O	D	T	O	H	D	P	G	O	D	P	A	L
D	I	P	D	E	T	Y	B	T	G	N	I	V	O	L
I	N	W	Y	O	D	S	P	A	Y	O	G	N	G	B
N	U	U	O	L	G	A	G	P	T	P	G	T	N	R
I	R	M	H	N	O	F	T	B	U	H	E	S	P	G
O	S	G	N	S	D	F	S	R	A	P	E	B	T	N
I	I	R	I	A	H	E	R	I	W	D	R	G	N	I
T	N	O	G	R	C	C	R	A	N	E	G	I	A	W
G	G	O	G	I	T	T	A	F	E	H	I	E	M	O
A	O	M	I	I	A	I	I	D	U	F	D	N	R	H
R	D	I	G	P	W	O	I	P	T	L	E	P	E	S
C	X	N	N	E	M	N	M	Y	E	H	P	T	G	R
E	O	G	D	G	G	A	T	I	R	L	N	X	D	E
N	I	D	T	E	E	T	H	I	N	G	G	G	P	G
L	R	D	O	X	I	E	T	C	H	P	E	R	E	N

AFFECTIONATE	PET	BADGERS
PUPPY	BATH	SHOWING
BREEDING	SMOOTH	CHAMPION
SPAY	DOG	TEETHING
DACHSHUND	WATCHDOG	DOXIE
WEINER	GERMAN	WIRE HAIR
GROOMING	WONDERFUL	HOTDOG
LAPDOG	LONG HAIR	LOVING
NEUTER	NURSING	PEDIGREE

Other Books Available by This Author

Woofing it Down – The Quick & Easy Guide to Making Healthy Dog Food At Home

Lapping it Up – The Quick & Easy Guide to Making Healthy Cat Food At Home

The Ultimate Yorkshire Terrier Book

The Ultimate Dachshund Hound Book

Tales of the Whosawhachits – Key Holder of the Realms – Book 1 (Young Adult)

Tales of the Whosawhachits – Enter the 5th Realm – Book 2 (Young Adult)

The Naughty Ones (Children's)

Mirror Mirror Seven Years Bad Luck (Adult Paranormal Fantasy)

COMING SOON

Tales of the Whosawhachits – Invasion of the Realms – Book 3 (Young Adult)

True Encounters with Imaginary Friends (Young Adult Novel)

The Ultimate Chihuahua Book

CPSIA information can be obtained at www.ICGtesting.com
Printed in the USA
BVOW070322080212

282451BV00003B/184/P